Turning
on the
Light

Finding your *Sweet Place* in the Spirit

WENDY DEWAR HUGHES

Turning
on the
Light

Finding your *Sweet Place* in the Spirit

WENDY DEWAR HUGHES

SUMMER BAY PRESS

Summer Bay Press

Copyright 2012 © Wendy Dewar Hughes

This book is a work of non-fiction though some fictional stories have been included for illustration purposes. Certain names, places and incidents have been changed in order to protect privacy. Any resemblance to actual events, locales, organizations, political groups, or persons, living or dead, is entirely coincidental and beyond the intent of the author or publisher.

Published by Summer Bay Press
#14 – 1884 Heath Road, Agassiz, B.C. Canada V0M 1A2

www.summerbaypress.com

Interior Design and Cover Design by Wendy Dewar Hughes, Summer Bay Press

Edited by Julene Hodges Schroeder, Editing Excellence

ISBN: 978-1-927626-03-0
Digital ISBN: 978-1-927626-04-7

To my good husband,
Gordon Hughes.
Thank-you for everything.
I couldn't do this without you.

TURNING ON THE LIGHT

Contents

How to use this book

The purpose of the book is to bring you into a closer relationship with your Creator. You may be someone who has no previous background in spiritual matters and is searching for answers and meaning to what is going on in your life. Or, you may be one who has just been introduced to spiritual concepts or a relationship with God and want to better understand how to make the most of this new found place in which you find yourself.

Wherever you are in your spiritual life, Turning on the Light will help you get a clearer picture of what a spiritual relationship with God can be like. Each chapter is designed to address a different step on the journey to a life of spiritual fulfillment. I have used illustrations from my own life, or fictional situations to portray the concepts.

At the end of each chapter you will find Journal pages which ask a series of questions that will help you apply the concepts to your own life. Please write in the book.

For the sake of simplicity, rather than using interchangeable terms such as Universe, Great Spirit, or terms from religious traditions, I have used the name God to refer to the Creator. I have chosen not to capitalize pronouns such as he, him, his, and for the sake of simplicity refer to God in the male gender only. If you would like to do a study on the names of God, you will find that some are more feminine than masculine but it really doesn't matter. God is a spirit and we have all been created in his image, so he clearly possesses qualities that both genders share.

I have used examples from my own life as illustrations whenever appropriate. Personal stories help to show how God works and how an ordinary person can have her life changed by his power and love. I have included excerpts from my own conversations with God that I have recorded in my journals over the years. These passages are in italics.

I hope that by reading about my experiences and the other stories in this book you will be inspired with the courage and desire to go after God's very best for your life.

ONE
Beginning

Each winter for the past several years I have travelled to Toronto to attend a trade show and buy products for a little gift and cheese store in which I am a partner. The shows take place near the end of January, unfortunately not the loveliest month to visit most Canadian cities. My brother, Brad, lives in a municipality adjoining the city of Toronto and near the site of the show that I attend.

One year, more than a month before my trip, I had arranged with Brad for him to pick me up from the airport when I arrived and that I would be able to stay at his house for the duration of my time there. When we talked, he told me that he and his family would be away until Thursday of that week so if I arrived on Friday or after, there would be no problem for him to pick me up and for me to stay at his home. I made my plans accordingly.

Before I was to fly to Toronto, I had just returned from a business trip to Atlanta, Georgia, so my mind was occupied with catching up on my business after being away and preparing for my upcoming Toronto trip.

A few days before my departure, I was talking with my mother on the telephone, "Brad's not going to be home when you get there," she told me. What? I had booked my flights to coincide with his travel plans. This was unwelcome news that could really throw off my travel plans.

I managed to contact my brother by email just before he left home. It seemed he had forgotten all about my visit when he and his wife booked their trip. At this late date, because of ticketing restrictions, rescheduling flights for either of us was out of the question.

After several emails back and forth, Brad arranged to leave his vehicle at an airport Park and Fly for me to pick up when I arrived in the city. In it he would also leave a bottle of water (which turned out to be frozen solid), the back end full of carpentry tools (he was renovating) and instructions how to get from the airport to his house (four pages including maps printed off the internet). Oh, and he had moved since I my previous visit.

My flight arrived into Toronto airport after 11:00 p.m. and in a snowstorm. By the time I got through baggage claim and reached the vehicle, it was well after midnight. The parking attendants had brushed most of the snow from the car but I had to let the engine run to get everything warmed up before I could begin to drive. At the time, I wore one contact lens which worked perfectly for me to see in broad daylight but makes it difficult to focus in low light. Reading Brad's directions in the dark was next to impossible. And there were lots of instructions.

Thus began my adventure.

I managed to follow the directions out of the parking lot and onto the nearest freeway. Driving in a snowstorm in a strange city at night on a freeway is not a good time to try to flip pages looking for instructions. Fortunately, because of the weather and the late hour, there was little traffic but I soon abandoned trying to both drive and read in favour of just keeping the vehicle on the road and moving forward.

Given that I had no idea where I was, what direction I faced, or where I should end up, I put myself entirely under the management of God for guidance. There was nowhere to stop and ask for directions and I had no GPS. Speaking to God directly, I asked him to show me exactly where to turn and in what direction to drive. I had no other way to find my destination.

As I drove along the freeway and read the signs indicating each exit, I mentally checked to see if it seemed like the right place to turn. After each exit that did not seem right, I continued to the next. Finally, an exit came up that seemed like the right place to turn. I turned on my signal light and left the freeway then pulled into the parking lot of a small shopping centre. Everything was closed up for the night. Snow swirled around the car as I stopped under a streetlight to take another look at the maps. Now I seemed more lost than ever. No street names on the maps matched the few street signs I could see through the falling snow.

With a sigh, I set out again using only the direction of God as my guide. By now the clock showed almost 1:00 a.m. I hesitated at the driveway out of the shopping centre parking lot, once again asking God for direction, and waited for a sense of which way to go. The streets lay thick and slippery with new snow. The trees along the streets shielded me from the wind as I turned right onto the street and crept through unknown neighbourhoods waiting for indications where to go next. After a while I came to a main street whose name I recognized. I had been on that street in previous visits to my brother's other house but didn't recognize this particular intersection at all. Should I turn or go straight? If I should turn then which way?

As I asked these questions in my mind to the Spirit of God, I sensed again that I should turn right. It just felt like the correct way to go. Turning left or going straight ahead felt like the wrong way. At the next major intersection I again asked what to do and followed the inner sensing for direction.

Finally, I came to a road that was mentioned in Brad's directions but as I sat at the **T** intersection and read his instructions to turn left I had the distinct impression that it was the wrong way. However, following the directions on the paper, I turned left onto this road. After travelling for only a few blocks the sense that I was going the wrong way was so strong that I felt compelled to turn around and go back toward the way I had come. Once I made the decision and turned around, it felt right again.

Along the street I found a single business open, a donut shop with a drive-through window. At the window sat a police car! I wheeled in and parked in front of the restaurant, hopped out of my vehicle, and waved the police officer to a stop as he pulled away from the window. *He must know the neighbourhood*, I reasoned, and when I stuck my head in his open window to ask directions I saw that he had a GPS (Global Positioning System) in his car.

I pulled the crumpled sheets of instructions from my pocket and asked if he could direct me to the correct street.

"Sure," he replied, "that street is just down that way about eight blocks" – in the direction that had felt right to me.

I found the correct corner and turned left then made the next turn onto my brother's street. The house number was difficult to read but I finally deduced which house was the one and pulled off the street into what I hoped was the driveway. Brad had warned me to park near the street and to be careful walking to the house as the whole yard was filled with trenches bristling with vertical reinforcing rods waiting for a warm spell to have the concrete footings poured for his new addition. The place was virtually booby-trapped!

I followed faint tracks through the heavy snow on boards over trenches to the back of the house as directed, where the door was unlocked. A friend of my nephew was staying with the family but no one was home when I arrived. I dragged in my luggage, turned up the heat and found something to eat. I checked around the house for signs that I was in the right place then went to bed. My own onboard GPS (God's Positioning System) had led me right to the open door I was to find.

This story may seem far-fetched to some, and completely natural to others. I assure you that it is true. What I want to convey through this and the other stories and anecdotes in this book is that God is alive and well and interested in us. He is as concerned with the small details that we have to deal with as much as with the big issues. He is eager to be included in every part of our day-to-day lives and is pleased to become involved wherever we will invite or allow him.

God wants to answer our questions about what life is all about, how to succeed, how to spend our time; who to trust and who to avoid, why we have problems, how to love without restraint and all the other issues that we face. He wants to help us live better, more fulfilled lives, and to give his directions and instruction for achieving the best life possible. And he wants us to know how much he loves us and cares about us.

This God is not a silent God. Many people have concluded that God must be silent since they have not been able to hear his voice or to penetrate what they see as a barrier between themselves and God. A relationship with God that is personal and meaningful seems totally out of reach.

Sometimes these barriers are real. We erect them ourselves by choosing to keep God out of our lives. Other times, the barriers are only imagined because we have not learned to understand how, when, and why he speaks to us and what he wants us to know. We just can't seem to get past the silence. We have not learned to discern the voice of our loving God.

My purpose in creating this program is to lead you into a better understanding of what God is like and to help you learn how you can access divine direction for your own life. What follows is a detailed explanation based on my own private quest to know and hear God, which has gone on for most of my life. Over the course of years my journey has taken many twists and turns but through it all, my desire to be acquainted with God has been the consuming quest of my life.

As I have sought God, I have found him and have steadily grown to grasp the magnitude of his unfathomable love. I know I still have a long way to go. We all have. We are, in a sense, fellow seekers of the deeper things of the spirit. As I have sought to hear God more and more clearly for myself, I have learned how he speaks in a noisy world and how to stay connected to him in spite of a busy mind and a schedule that is frequently overwhelming.

With diligence, practice, determination and patience, I have learned how to differentiate between the voice of God and that of my own spirit or mind. I have learned to recognize the difference between God's voice and the voices of the enemy spirits (also real) whose purpose is to divert us surreptitiously, with craft and guile, away from knowing and following God. As you proceed through the book you will learn that you can seek to hear from God so it is God's voice and his alone that you hear.

I want it to be clear that I am not advocating that you join any religion or church. Though I am presenting my subject primarily from a Christian perspective since that is my experience, you are not required to adhere to any of the tenets or beliefs of any particular church or doctrine in order to benefit from this material. I hope that you will set aside any pre-judgments or limiting beliefs as a result of past experiences in order to be open to receiving the information that I share. I assure you that your participation in any of the material in this program is entirely voluntary, but I encourage you to give yourself every opportunity to benefit from what it contains. I believe that living in close relationship with God provides great joy, fulfillment, and adventure. As spiritual beings, we must realize that the more we move into what God has in mind for each of us, the more exciting and dynamic life will be.

I will be using the Bible as my reference from time to time as I believe it is the most reliable document on record dealing with the character of God, how he interacts with people and what his purposes are for each of us.

You will find that I refer to God in different ways throughout this text so let me introduce you to some of the many names by which God is known.

First, there is simply, God. I believe that he is the creator of everything in the universe. When you ask "the universe" for something you want, or put your desire "out to the universe," it is God who picks up the message. Though there are many spirits operating in unseen realms in the universe (a subject we will discuss later) I do not believe that the universe has any power on its own or of its own. The power belongs to God. He is there to listen when you have a desire that your heart cries for or a wish that you dream of having fulfilled. He hears you when you call out for help in trouble and for comfort in pain or sorrow.

Then there is "the Father." The Bible refers often to God as a father. For many whose earthly experience has not included a worthy father figure, the concept of God as a loving father is sometimes difficult to grasp; perhaps it even seems impossible. I urge you to put aside your prior experiences with men who in the role of father have let you down, betrayed you, hurt you, or abandoned you. They have nothing whatever to do with God the Father. He is a father of a different ilk, cut out of a different cloth. God is your dream Dad. I encourage you, for the purpose of this book, to trade in your earthly father for the heavenly one. I will tell you how you can be adopted by the Father God. I believe you will discover as you learn about him, you will want to welcome him into your life as your new Father. When you do, I promise that you will never regret it.

God will also be referred to as "the Lord." The Bible uses this term frequently and I like it because it connotes an authority in my life, plus protective and defensive characteristics. Much like the lord of the manor is in charge of what happens on his land, including the protection of its boundaries and people, the Lord God is ready and willing to assume the same role in our lives.

Another way I may refer to God is "the Holy Spirit." Before Jesus' ministry ended with his crucifixion, he told his followers that it was better for everyone that he go away so that he could send the Comforter. The Comforter is another name for the Holy Spirit and a well-deserved one too, as we shall see. The Holy Spirit, or Comforter, is the Spirit of God here on earth. He cannot be seen with our physical eyes but his gentle presence can often very definitely be felt or sensed.

The Bible gives several other names when referring to God such as Wonderful, Counsellor, Prince of Peace, Everlasting Father, King of kings, plus God our strength, our healer, our hope, and more than six hundred other names reflecting his character and attributes.

With these few guidelines I invite you to embark with me on the voyage of discovery that has the power to change your life. Whether it does or not is up to you. I will provide the information and the tools for you to access God in a more intimate way than you may ever have before but you must do the work for it to work for you. I am convinced that when you do, you will enter into a whole new way of living and will never want to return to where you are today.

Throughout this text I will interject messages that I believe God has spoken directly to me. I have chosen these particular words from God from my own journals because I sense that he has instructed me to use them, and because they will help you to discern his voice and style of speech. They are also important messages to help in creating your relationship with God himself and to live a more successful and fulfilled life.

I will be referring to God, Jesus, and the Holy Spirit in the masculine gender for the sake of simplicity and because the Bible refers to them this way. If you want to do a study on the names of God, you will find that some are more feminine than masculine but it really doesn't matter. God is a spirit and we have all been created like him, so he clearly possesses qualities that both genders share.

I have tried to use examples from my own life as illustrations whenever possible. Personal stories help to show how God works and how an ordinary person can have her life changed by his power and love. I hope that by reading about my experiences and the other stories in the course, you will be inspired with the courage and desire to go after God's very best for your life.

Journal

In this introduction, I tell the story of how God led me to find my brother's house in an unfamiliar city in a snowstorm. Can you think of a time that you have sensed God leading you or when you have followed your intuition? Do you remember any times when you asked for God's help and then things "coincidentally" resolved or fell into place, almost miraculously? Write about one or two of those incidents here.

Think of another time when you followed your intuition or inner knowing or when you do so, on a regular basis, like finding a parking spot or meeting the right person. Tell about what happened and how it worked out. This exercise helps you to recognize that God is working in your life.

Have you had past experiences that caused you to doubt the existence of God? Write about any particular instances that caused you to come to conclusions about God that you would like to examine or question now.

Do you believe that there is a spiritual force in the universe, or that if you put your wishes or desired "out to the universe" there is a power there to cause what you wish for to come to pass? What do you call that power?

Do you feel ready to consider that there is a loving God of the universe? Would you be more comfortable with the idea of God if called by some other name, and if so, what might that name be? (For lists of the many names of God, try doing a Google search using "names of God" in the search line. You'll be amazed at the diversity.)

Do you ever feel that there are or have been barriers between you and God because of choices you have made in your past or situations that you are now involved with? Tell about that.

Do you believe that hearing God's voice is weird or spooky or that God only speaks to religious figures like priests, or pastors or other spiritual personalities? Would you like to learn how you can hear God yourself? Why?

In the introduction, I recommend that you put aside any prejudice regarding past teaching about God or the Bible so that you may be open to new information. If you have trouble with this, try to articulate it here as a means of identifying what limiting beliefs you may hold.

In order to achieve a deeper and more intimate relationship with God, it is important to be open to what he has to tell you and to give you. Even if you do not feel ready to take that step, by choosing to *be willing* to allow yourself to move closer to God and for him to speak to you, you are taking the first step to an abundant and beautiful experience of knowing God. If you have misgivings, or feel nervous about this step, write your reasons below. Would you be willing for God to help you to be willing to know him better?

TWO

Starting Out

Wouldn't it be wonderful if you could hear the voice of God yourself? Many people believe that is not possible, or that only a chosen few actually hear God. Lots of people believe that God spoke only to the long-bearded, calling-down-fire-from-heaven type of prophets, ages ago in Old Testament days. Some even hold the belief that only the mentally ill believe they hear God and those who claim they do should see a doctor, and soon. I can assure you that this is not the case. You don't have to be a head-case, wear a beard, or receive a special dispensation to hear God. Anyone can, including you.

Many earnest and honest individuals try desperately to discern what God may be trying to tell them about their lives, their problems, what choices to make and what direction to take. They seek for signs, feelings, circumstances, and even goose bumps that will give them some assurance of God's interest in their lives and problems, and direction for their paths. They often continue to seek without any real assurance that what is going on is part of God's plan or wonder if they have heard from God at all. Or they are not sure if what they think they heard was actually God, coincidence, their imagination, or just indigestion. Most are plagued by varying degrees of uncertainty and often give up looking for God's leading in their lives out of sheer frustration or bewilderment.

Those who have learned to hear and discern the voice of God are often reticent to reveal that we actually hear him speak to us because we feel that by doing so we are opening ourselves up to the skepticism, criticism or even ridicule of others. There are very few circles where hearing from God personally is accepted, understood, honoured or praised. I am breaking the silence about hearing God and sharing what I know and what I have found that works.

Hearing from God is not complicated or difficult. To set the stage for your journey to the heart of God, I will use the following metaphor to help you see where you may be now and where you will want to be in order to understand easily how God can lead in your life.

Imagine that you are on a basketball team and the big game is about to start. You have spent months practicing and honing your skills for just such a time as this. You have spent large amounts of time with your team-mates and with your coach, getting to know one another and learning the strategies you intend to use to win this game. Your coach is a pro and he instructs the team on how to work together to have victory over the opposing team. He understands how the coach of the other team thinks, what strategies that coach is likely to use against your team, and has a good idea of the strengths and weaknesses of the opposing team's players.

The bleachers bulge with cheering fans as you and your team prepare to enter the court. You know that you all have your moves down and are ready for the game, and as long as everyone follows the leading of your coach, victory could well be in your grasp.

Your team lopes out of the locker room and onto the court. The crowd leaps to its feet, screaming and waving pennants and pompoms. You are on the home court and the crowd's numbers are heavily weighted in your favour. The hands of the clock edge toward the starting time as you and your teammates take your seats along the side of the court.

The referees are in a huddle going over last minute regulations and synchronizing their watches. Across the court the other team troops in to a chorus of boos and hisses from all but a small percentage of the crowd, who, to make up for their limited numbers, go wild in an effort to drown out the noise from the home team crowd. The opposing team's players trot to their places along the far side of the court and sit down, each head bent toward the coach for last minute instructions and encouragement. You see them glare across the polished floor at your team, determination in their eyes. They plan to do everything in their power to see that your team is humiliated in defeat. They are here to win and to annihilate you and your team in the process.

Suddenly, a strange thing happens. It catches your eye and instantly captures your attention. As your attention shifts, your coach's voice fades to a mumble. The other players on your team may as well be in another country, so invisible have they become. The roar of the crowd diminishes as this peculiar scene begins to unfold. Your eyes are like lasers staring across that court now. You see the other team and their coach and you are gripped by the spectacle unfolding before you. One thought has taken control of your mind, your senses; in fact it seems like, your entire being is this: What on earth is that person doing?

In an instant, you realize that your team-mates have now seen it, too. You glance nervously at each other then turn as one to stare at the sight before you. The screams of the crowd have fallen to a hush as they stare, also now wondering what on earth is happening. The shrill blast from a referee's whistle fills the auditorium but it may as well be a train whistle in the night for the effect it has. What you see, what everyone sees, is the captain of the opposing team crossing the floor and approaching the bench of your team. One of your players alerts your coach whose head snaps round. His eyes narrow as he the approaching player.

The opposing team's captain marches up to your coach and stops, toe to toe. Your coach looks into the captain's chest then slowly raises his head to meet the eyes of this interloper.

"Hey," says the player from the other team, breaking into a grin. "How about bringing me up to speed on your plays? I want to play on your team for a bit, then I'll go back over there," indicating the other team, "and finish up the game with my pals."

Your team members blink. You coach regards this person steadily for a moment then says, "*Shipka gliraxi spelishina marfo ban isini kablinai.*"

"Huh?" The player stares at your coach then looks at you. "Wha'd he say?"

You rise to your feet. "He says you won't be able to understand the plays unless you join the team."

"Oh, no, no," the other player says, head shaking. "I don't want to do that. I still want to play on my own team. I just want your coach to tell me all the secret stuff he tells you guys."

The coach says something else that the player does not understand. You translate, "You are welcome to join our team, he says, but you'll have to quit playing with the opposition."

This is the point where this player must make a choice. Which team would be the best to play on? Will this team captain decide to remain with the team across the court, following the leading of their coach? They have a lot of fun at times, but at the end of the day, no one is very happy. The coach is unpredictable; in fact, sometimes downright miserable but always tries to make it up to the players by buying drinks, new jerseys or steak dinners for them.

Then again, switching teams might be a pretty good idea. The players on your team are in good shape, you work well as a team, and you win a lot of games. The coach is a likable guy; in fact in some circles, your coach, though tough, is known as the best in the business.

This opposing team's captain is uncertain. Playing with your team could be the chance of a lifetime, but it could mean giving up the free dinners. In these brief moments, the player tries to consider all options. What if playing on your team isn't what it's cracked up to be? How is he going to understand that coach when they clearly speak a different language? What if, once the choice has been made, there is no going back? On the other hand, what if it is so great that going back would no longer even be considered? The dilemma is choosing between the known but not satisfactory, and the unknown but possibly the best.

Learning to hear God's voice and knowing what he is saying for your specific circumstances is not unlike the situation in this story. Imagine that you are that player in the story who crosses the floor and you want something better for your life. You see that others seem to be connected to divine guidance and you would like to experience that, too. But you are not sure that you want to leave where you are and "cross the floor" to join a different team, a group that is doing something different than you have been doing and getting different results than you have been getting. You are not sure what will be required of you and if you will want whatever that may be.

If you feel like this, you are not alone. Many people would love to be able to get instructions for their lives from God but are unclear on how to go about it or afraid if they move in a more spiritual direction they may wind up in a situation they hadn't bargained for. As you work through this program, we will deal with those questions and fears so that you have a clear understanding about how to move into position to hear God and set boundaries that keep you safe.

To continue with the basketball metaphor, God is the coach of the team. In order to hear and understand the leading of the coach, you will have to spend time on the team, get to know the coach and learn how he speaks to his own players.

If you don't join the team you can't expect to be an insider when instructions come down from above. God could be speaking to you, and I believe he is, but without tuning in to how he speaks, you will not hear or understand a word he's saying. The first choice you must make to be able to hear the voice of God is to choose to be on his team. The invitation for you to join God's "team" is always open; in fact, you can join whenever you want to. You can also decline the invitation to be part of his family, but if you do, how will you hear him when he calls your name, has something to tell you, or offers to guide, protect, or help you? How will you recognize his answers to your pleas when you call on him in time of need or sorrow?

We all must, at some time in life, choose whom we will follow. You see, it doesn't work to play a little for one team, then switch to another, then hop the fence and go play for a third, because at the end of the game (which can happen at any time) you may not like where you end up. The most successful kind of life is one filled with purpose and direction. Yet many people do not make a conscious choice as to what they will believe, preferring to drift through life being blown to and fro by every wind of philosophy or doctrine that comes along. However, by not making a conscious choice to be led by God, you, by default, make the choice not to.

In the same way that you can't be sort of pregnant, or sort of unique, you can't sort of believe something. You either believe it or you do not. You are either in or out, on the team or not. There is no middle ground, no here one day, there the next, no hot then cold, in then out, up then down, no half-heartedness. To try to live in this wishy-washy, undecided way means never having a stable foundation upon which to build your life. If you consider that how you do one thing is how you do everything, how then will you have stability in any area of your life? At some point we all have to make the decision how we will live our lives. You can't choose to believe sometimes and not at other times if you want to know God well.

Now you might be asking, "Why do I have to choose anything? I'm a free agent, independent, self-reliant. I don't need anyone. I will live my own way, do my own thing, and be my own boss." Well, you can do that, sure, but you will never hear God that way. God won't force you to take the time to get to know him. He will never impose his will on you, never take you by the shoulders and give you a shake to get your attention. Your attentiveness to his leading is entirely your own choice. We all have a free will and the choice to go through life however we choose. You may even think that you can go through life as a spectator, never really choosing any particular path, just staying out of everyone's way, but you would be wrong again. In life there are no spectators, only participants. Don't forego the opportunity you have for a relationship with God. One day it may be too late.

Or you might be saying, "I'm a good person. I don't lie, cheat, steal or hurt anyone. Why wouldn't God want to speak to me?" God does want to speak to you and has actually been speaking to you all along. But until you align your own life with his plans for you, you will continue to miss hearing his voice. It is rather like a student who wants to learn a new language. Unless she enrolls in a class, pays her tuition, buys and studies the text, attends the classes, and does her assignments, she can't expect to learn to speak the language, can she?

At some time we have all had questions like those above. You do good deeds, don't yell at your kids (well, not much, anyway), come home every night, drive the speed limit, (except when you have to "keep up with the traffic" or you're in a hurry). You might volunteer on the cancer run, look after your aging parents, keep a clean house and pay your bills on time. While doing things like these may make for a better life and a better world for us all to live in, comparing these types of activities to positioning yourself to hear God's voice, is like comparing feathers to sardines. Performing good deeds bears no relation to the question at hand.

The reason is that doing things cannot qualify us to be part of God's circle of confidants, simply because God is perfect and we are not. There is a fundamental disconnect between God and us, and no matter how hard I try, how good I attempt to become, or what state of enlightenment I feel I have attained, I can never resolve that disconnect through any performance on my part. Put simply, God is so perfect and I am so imperfect, that try as I might, on my own I can never become perfect enough to connect with God. That's a rather shocking realization, isn't it?

It means that even though I may not lie habitually, if I have ever lied in my life, I have already blown it. I may not cheat on my taxes, but if I have ever cheated on a test, or didn't correct the cashier when I knew she gave me the wrong change, then I have disqualified myself from the perfection that God's inner circle requires. Whether a person has committed the most heinous crime or is the sweetest grandmother who just never forgave someone forty years ago, it still all chalks up to the same thing. On our own, we cannot achieve that intimate closeness with God that allows us to know the sound of his voice and understand what he has to say.

However, before you begin to despair, I am happy to say there is an answer. In fact, the solution to the dilemma of the "disconnect" is as simple as it is profound. There is a way to overcome this limitation and disqualification, a way to become the perfection that we must be in order to be one with God. There is only one way, but that one way is all we need. In one easy, life-changing step, we can make the change that positions us forever as part of God's inner circle and allows us to begin to hear him speak into our lives.

Before I go any further, let me tell you a bit about my own experience. In my family in which I grew up and in attending Sunday School and church as a child, I realized that God speaks to some people. I met individuals who seemed to know God very well and had an intimate relationship with him, to the point of disclosing conversations they had shared with God, and personal guidance they had received. I was fascinated with these people and their stories about their contacts with God. It sounded so wonderful and the more I learned about God and how he interacted with others, the more I wanted that for my life, too.

As a sensitive and intuitive child, I was always aware of the spiritual side of life, but it took me a long time and some earnest study to understand that just being aware that I have a spirit, or just being a good person, were not enough to place me in a position to grasp what friendship with God could really be like.

As a young adult I took this knowledge and set about to study different spiritual practices, religions, and methods. After some years of searching, I came to realize that the message of the Bible is not just a collection of stories about ancient people, but a series of accounts and letters that God had compelled certain of his followers to write throughout history in order to provide a guidebook for those who came after, for living a successful and spiritually alive life. The more I studied these accounts, the greater my understanding became of how to relate to God in a way that would allow me to enjoy conversations with him like others whom I had admired.

Step by step, year by year, I moved into the relationship in which I now take such pleasure. I view where I am today as on a continuum that leads me to an ever closer and more intimate relationship with God. I can't say that I never get things wrong, or that I am not occasionally confused, but by and large, I now quite easily hear the voice of God. When I seek direction or guidance, I have the assurance that God not only wants to help me with decisions but he hears my requests, answers my questions, and he gives me the information I need to create a purposeful and significant life that is fulfilling for me and pleasing to God.

So how do you find this seemingly elusive relationship for yourself? What do you have to do, be, or change in order to bridge the gap between where you are and intimacy with the divine? The answer is summed up in one word. Believe.

Becoming part of God's inner circle is not a complicated procedure; in fact, it is quite straightforward. You need make only one choice in order to position yourself to hear from God. That choice is whether or not to believe. By choosing to believe, you establish yourself as a child of God, part of God's family. By choosing not to believe, you exempt yourself from God's inner circle.

But believe what, exactly?

We all must come to the realization some time, that there is more to life than just what we see with our eyes. Something in us knows there is more than just getting a good job, having a family, a house in the suburbs, or the city, or the country. There is much more to life than going to work every day, coming home for supper, watching television and going to bed, then getting up in the morning and doing it all again.

If you live like this, sooner or later your spirit will become disquieted within you. It might happen when you wake in the still of the night while your spouse is asleep beside you and the moonlight or the light from a streetlamp shines through your window casting deep shadows in the corners of your room. Maybe it will happen when you see your newborn child, or when someone you love dies, or when you realize that in spite of everything you do and no matter how busy you are, you are still profoundly lonely. Perhaps you will have a near-death experience like a car crash, or a medical emergency that nearly takes your life. These kinds of experiences bring us up short and cause us to evaluate what life is really about. There comes such a time in each person's life, often more than once if you continue to sit on the fence. It may not be cataclysmic or earthshaking. It may only be one day coming home too tired to see straight, when you spirit speaks up on the inside of you and says, "Well?"

These times can be pretty scary. Has this happened to you? You have looked deep inside yourself for a brief moment and what you saw or didn't see frightened you so much that you didn't want to go there again. So rather than looking for answers, you medicate yourself with constant activity, sex, drugs or alcohol, unfulfilling relationships, a packed work schedule, or anything you can think of that will dull the ache or assuage the fear. The fear is either that there is a lot more to life than you are experiencing and you feel so off-base that you will never find it, or that there is no more to life and this is it. You don't want to ask yourself if this empty cavern of need or sorrow or loneliness is the best you can expect. If you did, what then?

You may have gone searching for answers, more meaning, even for truth and have found something that seems to be it. You hear lots of people talking about "spirit" and "the universe" and you think, *Hey, they seem to have it figured out,* so you do what they do. You read the books, go to the latest guru or ashram or retreat or support group. For a while it's great. You have these neat friends who are all so aware of the spiritual realm, maybe even channelling spirit "guides," or talking to their own personal angels, or using crystals to connect with spiritual entities who promise power, healing, wealth and peace. Someone may even have led you to invite a spirit guide or angel to speak to you, or have influence in your life. If you have gone through any of these experiences, and have been left more confused than ever, or not sure that you have found the truth, this program will help to clear the fog for you. If you were not already spiritually sensitive, you would not be embarking on this course, so some of these things are very good.

What you will read and hear in what follows will help you to find a way through all the noise and spiritual confusion to the truth that God has for you. If you have been hearing voices from the spirit world, you will need to tell those voices to be quiet for a while as we go through the program. In the interest of enjoying the best possible results, I urge you to make the decision now to put all previously learned spiritual thinking aside for the moment. It is important that you be single-minded and focused for the duration of the course. Later on, you will want to bring that back out and examine it in light of your new knowledge and experience.

Before you jump to the conclusion that believing just about anything about God will achieve these results, let me warn you that this is decidedly not so. There are many teachings and messages in the world today whose sole purpose is to counterfeit truth. In some instances, the teachers of these doctrines may not even be aware that they are the purveyors of falsehoods, being themselves deceived.

You must realize that there is an enemy spirit afoot whose sole aim is to steer you away from truth, to deceive you and to lead you away from God. You see, there are really only two teams or spheres of influence at work in the spiritual world. These two are the force of good and the force of evil. Just as God is a real presence and personality for good, rather than just some kind of amorphous universal feeling, the force of evil is also a real presence. To use the biblical definition, the personality that is the force of evil is called Satan, or the devil, and is a real spiritual force. Now, don't panic, because God, the force of good, is so much more powerful than evil, that evil can be overcome – if you know how. We will deal with the presence of evil influence later in the program, so please stay with me. I will show how it is not difficult to recognize the force of evil at work in your life, and to overcome it before it wreaks havoc with you.

When we have finished the course, you will have a clear and definite basis for comparison on which to build your belief systems and your life. I am convinced that by the time you have worked through this program, you will have a different outlook on your spiritual life than when you began.

The main concept we all must remember is that God is good. He is a God of love. The good stuff in life comes from God, not the bad stuff. Too many people have it all mixed up. The bad stuff comes from the other side, namely the devil. If you get this part figured out right, you are almost there. The good stuff in life comes from God; the bad stuff comes from the devil. Remember that and don't get them confused! This is a rule to live by.

Now I will tell you how you can make sure that you choose the right beliefs so that you may obtain a place in the family of God. As I said before, none of us is perfect enough as we are to meet with God. But God loves us so much, that he determined a way to bridge the gap between himself and us. Basically, God couldn't face an eternity without company so he has provided a way for us to appear before him as perfect in his eyes, even though we are not and can never attain perfection on our own.

You see, God provided a perfect scapegoat for us who agreed to appear before God on our behalf. This stand-in, or go-between, is Jesus, and he stands in the gap between our imperfection and God's perfection and takes our place. By accepting Jesus as our stand-in, as our placeholder, we become eligible to stand before God. In essence, Jesus goes before God in our place, and acts as our perfection so we have the access to God that would otherwise be denied.

What am I saying? Simply this: We must choose to believe that Jesus is our go-between, he is the conduit that connects us to God and opens the channels for us to become friends with God and to truly hear his voice. Jesus is the one who makes us right before God. He is the one who stands in our place when we know that we've totally missed the mark, blown it big time, lived a life of little value, or just feel rotten. Jesus is the only one who can deal with all of our offences, misdeeds, transgressions, faults and errors, clean us up internally and make us appear perfect in the eyes of God. It's mind-boggling, I know, but that's why it takes faith – why we have to choose to believe. We can't figure it out on our own nor accomplish it by ourselves.

To have a relationship with Jesus is to have a relationship with God since they are different manifestations of the same spirit. The concept of the trinity is a difficult one to grasp, but is best compared to us. We each have a body, a soul (mind, will, emotions) and are a spirit (the real you, the part the makes you alive). So we also resemble a trinity. I don't want to dwell on this concept, except to say that in a relationship with God, we also have a relationship with Jesus Christ, and with the Holy Spirit. It's all good. This is what God says:

> *Sometimes you must step out in faith for my will to come to pass in your life. You must let go of the safety handles and let yourself be carried by my Spirit.*

Align yourself with Truth. The Word of God contains all the truth you will ever need to live a prosperous and successful life. The first step in knowing and hearing God is to do what the Word of God says to do. Jesus used the analogy of himself as a shepherd and his followers as his sheep when he said, "My sheep hear my voice." If you want to hear from God the first step is to become like one of Jesus' sheep. To do that, you must make the choice to believe that Jesus is the Son of God and that God sent him to earth to save you from spending eternity separated from him. As humans, our bodies will one day die, but the spirit in you will live forever. Eternal separation from God and all that he has for you is a horrible place and you don't want to go there, so you must take steps now to avert that possibility.

I urge you not to miss the opportunity of a lifetime by making the choice to follow God now. Don't wait until later, until you've had time to think it over, or until the dishes are done. Making the choice is simple. You can say something like, "I am making the choice that from now on I will believe in God, and I also believe that Jesus made it possible for me to connect with God. Thank you." It is important to recognize that it was Jesus who made it possible for us to have a close and personal relationship with God, and to thank him for being our go-between.

God will hear you and honour your decision. You can begin right now to have a relationship of intimacy with God that will totally transform your life and lead you to joys that you have never known before.

If there were only one path for your life, the choice would be easy. You would not have to pause to consider which the right path is, or of two right paths, which is the most right path. If there were only one path, you would not be required to choose. But life is full of possibilities. It is full of choices. I set before you a myriad of choices and say, "Choose this day whom you will follow." For the first and most important choice is to choose to follow me.

Journal

In this chapter we discuss how you can join God's 'inner circle' and become eligible to live your life in close personal relationship with him. In your experience have you, or someone you know, ever attempted to figure out what God is doing but been unable to understand exactly why things happen as they do? Try to describe one or more of those experiences here.

Describe a time in your life when you have asked for God's help or guidance. Are you able to see how God may have helped you through that situation? How?

In the metaphor of the basketball game, can you visualize yourself in this setting? Even if competitive team sports are not your interest, can you identify with the player who wants to hear from the coach yet cannot understand what he says? Describe any experience you may have had when you hoped to hear God speak to you, but were left uncertain and confused about the response or lack of it.

If you have sought to hear God speak to you in the past, does this metaphor help you to understand where the source of your difficulty may lie? Try to look at your life in terms of whose 'team' you have been on. As this story illustrates, it is not possible to play on both teams on a basketball court any more than it is possible to live your life as a believer and an unbeliever at the same time. How does knowing that make you feel?

In your experience until now, have you been aware that you must make the choice to be on 'God's team', that it may not be automatic? What beliefs have you held that support or oppose this concept?

Now that you are aware that besides God, who is the force for good, there is a force of evil operating in the world, I'm sure you can see how understanding this may dramatically affect your life. By choosing to side with God and inviting him to take an active part in your life, can you see how this positions you to hear him?

It's true that you might have difficulty hearing God if you do not choose to be a believer. Take a little time to examine your choices as described in the book, and write your thoughts here.

Have you, like me, spent time exploring other spiritual beliefs, customs and philosophies? To what degree have you found that these philosophies have impacted your life? Have any of these practices drawn you into a closer, more intimate knowledge and experience with God or have they left you more confused and uncertain? How?

To build your life on a firm foundation it is necessary to resolve what you truly believe. Once you have settled that, it is much easier to move forward and to make important decisions that shape your life. As a believer, your life is based on God's word and his plans for you. With this in mind, tell how your life might change as you begin to include God in your decisions and plans.

As humans, we at some time may come to the place in our lives where we wonder if there is more to life than just our daily activities and relationships. Describe a time or instance when you have had similar thoughts or speculations. How did you feel during those times? How do you feel about them now?

It is not unusual for people to use a variety of methods to dull pain, chase away boredom, or mask our fears. Think about your life now and see if you can identify ways that you may now or in the past have used overwork, drugs or alcohol, relationships, or other means to avoid looking deep inside yourself. Write down your thoughts about this.

If you have sought answers to your spiritual questions, have you found yourself uncertain whether what you have learned is the truth? What have you learned about spiritual matters so far that you may need, as suggested in the book, to put aside for the moment?

The concept that God is good and is not out to get you is a new idea for some people. If this has been your attitude toward God, it is important to suspend that belief now. Write down all the negative beliefs you have had or have learned about God here.

Now that you have this list, put a big X through it all and write the word, LIES, in big letters across it. Whenever those old beliefs come back to interfere with your believing in the goodness of God check back with your list and remind yourself that they are only lies.

Some people have trouble believing that there is a spirit of evil called Satan, or the devil. Now that you know that the good in life comes from God and the bad or evil stuff comes from this devil, can you see how these two powers are in effect in the world around us. List some events you know about where you can clearly see God's hand at work, or the hand of evil.

It is impossible for us to be perfect enough on our own to be friends with God, so Jesus was offered as our go-between. When we choose to believe in Jesus as our advocate and friend, this choice changes our lives forever. Making that choice is a simple matter of thinking a new thought and saying it out loud. I suggest something like this: "Jesus, I make the choice now to believe in you and to accept that you make it possible for me to know God and to hear him speak to me. I invite you now to come into my life, and to become my friend and my very own advocate with God. Thank-you." I urge you to take some time to think about this choice you have made and to write down how you feel about making this choice.

THREE

Spending the time

Have you ever had the experience of wanting a second opinion but had no one to ask? Since I own a business, I spend a lot of time alone writing, designing, and working in my office. I often need someone to talk things over with, but no one is there. Of course, I have an assistant who comes in when I need her, joint venture partners, business contacts, and consultants with whom I work from time to time, but by choice I spend most days entirely by myself.

There are also times when I am away from my office, travelling, running errands, shopping, or making calls, and I think it would be nice to have someone with whom I could talk things over – someone who could remind me of what I might miss. It seldom occurs to me to phone a friend or relative for ideas or input because I don't want to bother or interrupt others about small decisions. Usually when I need a second opinion there is simply no one available.

I recall one day when I was shopping for shoes. I needed a new pair of plain walking shoes since I had worn the lining right out of my old ones. I had managed to find a day to fit in a shopping trip since the shoe situation had reached crisis proportions. Sandal weather was coming to an end. I had prolonged the season as long as possible, but now my feet were starting to get cold.

I chose to visit a mall in a city over an hour's drive away, where I had some business to conduct. In the department stores I checked, I found nothing, so I wandered down the mall, perusing the variety available in all of the shoe stores. I finally found a pair of shoes that fit quite well, though not perfectly, and they cost more than I wanted to pay. Finding shoes to fit is always a challenge because my feet are wide across the knuckles, long in the toes, high in the arches, and narrow in the heels. Generally, if the shoes are wide enough not to pinch, they are too long for me and too loose in the back, so I am used to wearing shoes that don't quite fit since so few are contoured to fit my foot shape.

As I walked around the store in this particular pair of shoes, I felt uncertain about whether I should buy them. They would probably be adequate for what I needed, but were somewhat stiff and might not be comfortable enough for walking any distance. I was shopping alone, and as we all know, the store clerks cannot be relied upon for unbiased opinions, so I silently asked the Lord what I should do. Immediately, the answer came back to me, "Don't buy these. Keep looking."

I returned the shoes to the clerk and thanked her for her help then continued down the mall. Nearing the end of the mall, I turned in to another shoe store, which had a pretty sizable selection from which to choose. I tried on a few pairs. One style fit me beautifully. These ones were made of soft leather, had cushioned insoles and felt as comfortable as slippers. When I asked the price, the clerk informed me that they were on sale that day for twenty-five percent off the regular price. I knew that these were the ones that God had picked out for me, knowing my needs, my feet and my budget. I promptly bought them. These shoes have outlasted most of the other shoes I have owned because they fit me perfectly from the start. I was delighted with my purchase and God's help in finding me the right shoes to buy.

This might seem like an inconsequential incident, but I share it to demonstrate that God is not only able, but also willing to help with the smallest details that concern us. Finding the right shoes at the right time helped me a lot. It saved me time and energy, not to mention some money. I take such pleasure and satisfaction in knowing God and feel such joy knowing that I can hear him when I need his help. He continually makes my life easier and better.

The scriptures record repeated incidents where individuals heard from God directly, clearly, concisely and definitely, in all kinds of situations. Time and again, people who sought God made the connection with him and God spoke to them in ways that were simple and easy to understand.

The Bible also says that God is no respecter of persons, which means that no one is born to a position greater or lesser than yours or mine. I don't have to be "somebody" or hold some lofty ranking in order to talk to God and to hear him talk to me. In fact, he is not the least bit impressed by worldly position or titles. Royalty has no more pull with him than has a beggar. That is because God does not look at outward appearances. He regards the inner person.

Through my studies I came to realize that if God does not esteem anyone more or less than me, and if he spoke to others, then he would also speak to me. This is great news! To know that I am never disqualified from hearing God based on my station in life, my relationships, my past, my career, or any other reason, means that I am right now in the position to hear God's voice. If that is the case, then it is simply a matter of learning how. Over the years as I have diligently sought God and found that he does speak to ordinary people like me, often in very ordinary ways, yet what he says makes a profound difference in the how I live. When I call on him he hears, he listens, and he answers.

It has been many years since I embarked on my quest to learn to hear God for myself. What led to my final decision to pursue him and not give up until I was satisfied was a family tragedy. My heart was aching and needed comfort. Nice words and platitudes weren't helping. Sympathy, though momentarily soothing, didn't last nor did it answer my questions.

From this place of sorrow, I recognized that I must find out how to become one of those who could hear God, because I knew that I could no longer be content with weak, bland religious clichés or meaningless emotional condolences. It's not that I don't care for sentimentality; it's just that I had come to the place that I could no longer settle for it. It wasn't working. I found little comfort in the commiseration of others. I needed answers and I needed to know that they were coming from God. I had to go to the source of comfort and knowledge himself.

From my background of going to Sunday School and church all my childhood, I knew that God spoke to people in the Bible in a variety of ways, so I set out to learn more about them and to see which ones would work for me. I had heard people talk about how God spoke to them (usually missionaries) and I wanted to be one of those people who consistently heard and understood his voice.

I knew, for example, that one way God often spoke to people was through dreams. You can find a good example of this in the story of baby Jesus, when King Herod, the ruler at that time, wanted him killed.

God spoke to Jesus' earthly father, Joseph, in a dream and told him to get up and take his family to Egypt to be safe from the king's henchmen. When the danger had passed, Joseph had another dream in which God told him that it was safe to return to Israel. To Joseph, these dreams were so clearly God speaking to him, that he responded instantly.

Though I have very clear dreams, and almost always wake with a vivid recollection of what I've been dreaming, I knew (though God had communicated with me this way before) this was not the only method he could use. I knew there would be times when I would need God's direction at any waking moment and it would be imperative for me to learn to discern his voice every day. A dream wouldn't help me if I was stuck in traffic, had an appointment, or needed to know an alternate route in an unfamiliar neighbourhood. I wanted to be able to talk to and hear God all the time.

Another method God used to communicate with people was to send an angel to relay a message, give a warning, or answer people's questions. The Bible records many instances when angels appeared, delivering messages and bringing help from God. In those days, people did not find it surprising when they heard of the appearance of an angel.

Though not as common, God also sometimes speaks to people in an audible voice. You and I are more likely to "hear" his voice as an inner nudge, a sense of conscience, a certain knowing, a definite impression, or actual words spoken into our minds. Sometimes God speaks through dreams, visions, or circumstances when we are unable to get alone and quiet with him long enough to hear the still, small voice he uses to speak within us. However, the more time we spend with God, the more familiar his voice will become and the more we will hear actual words spoken into our minds or hearts, or even our ears.

In my studies, I have learned that many people just had conversations with God, and he gave them instructions when they needed or asked for his direction. They talked to him, and he talked back. I wanted that.

I found that God wants to answer our questions – questions as big as the meaning of life to as simple as what to cook for supper or what to wear for a meeting. God has all the answers. He has answers as to why we have a sickness and how to get well, how to make good business decisions, how to prioritize our commitments to avoid undue stress, how to treat others in relationships, and everything else. In short, God is interested. He cares about every aspect of our lives. He wants to be completely involved, to help, lead and guide, comfort, befriend, heal, protect and defend. He has a lot to say about success, money, debt, service, and time-management. He wants to teach us how to relax, to dream, to have joy and to endure difficult times. He speaks and he wants us to hear, listen and respond.

So if God wants to speak to us, why are we not all hearing him regularly? How is it that some people seem to hear God easily and others think they never hear God's voice at all? Why do some people struggle to understand how a dynamic relationship with God works and remain confused when it comes to hearing him speak? Is it easy or difficult to communicate with God?

Because of my own experiences, studies, and the relationship I enjoy with God, I want to help you learn how you can hear his voice for yourself when you need to and for whatever reason. My own private mission to hear God easily, consistently and confidently has gone on for more than forty years. Please don't assume that it will take you that long. I now know that it needn't have taken me that long either and by the end of this course you, too, should be able to have daily conversations with God.

I am so thankful that I persisted in getting to know God and learning to hear him, because this relationship has given me more peace, joy, hope, and love than I could ever have imagined. I am convinced that you will find the same for your life.

Let's begin with the easiest method for discovering God's desires for you and his guidelines for success. God has provided an excellent manual for us to use. Even though this book is easy to obtain, many people have only minimal familiarity with it, which is surprising because it is the world's all-time bestseller. The guidebook is the Bible and it contains texts written and gathered over the centuries, drawn from the experiences of many, many people and includes their dialogues with God. These texts have been collected and consolidated into two main sections, making up one book. The Old Testament details historical events and people's experiences that took place before Christ's birth, and the New Testament chronicles Jesus' time on earth followed by the acts and experiences of his closest followers.

A lot happened before Christ was born. Over thousands of years, people just like you and me sought a closer relationship with God, and dedicated themselves to knowing him and understanding his ways. History is full of conflicts and wars, peace and calm, anguish and love, birth and death, and struggle and triumph. You will find all these issues and more in the pages of the Bible. You will also find how God interacted with mankind, what he said, how he controlled nature, how helped his followers to defeat their foes and aided in the victories of those who called themselves his own. If you read carefully, you will find that God always honoured those who revered him, whose hearts were open to his leading and who, no matter what mistakes they made, always returned to his love. When you read, pay special attention to how God treated those who placed themselves under his care.

Though it may require some study to understand parts of these texts, let me urge you to begin to read them regularly. Unlike the written words of any other book or text, the words of the Bible contain a direct link to the Spirit of God. God infused his words with his *power*, so that when you read them, they have an impact that is unequalled by any other writings. By reading and applying God's word in your life, you directly access his power and wisdom for yourself. I cannot explain how this happens except that it is supernatural.

If you don't already own a Bible, I urge you to get one, preferably a modern-day language version so that you can easily understand from his own book how God works. Biblical scholars have combed the scriptures in the original languages to provide accurate translations of the original meanings.

The great thing about reading the Bible is that you don't have to start at the beginning. You can start reading anywhere and you will always find something important that you can apply to your own life. When reading, especially in the Old Testament, remember my illustration about the basketball teams. The way God dealt with people who chose to follow him was vastly different from those who steadfastly rejected him. That same applies today. When you choose to be a member of God's team, it affords a lot of benefits not available to those who reject God. God will still love and care for you just as much if you reject his overtures of love, but you will miss out on the countless perks that come to those who choose to follow God.

We all know that some things never change and this is why the Bible is as relevant and pertinent today as it has ever been. Human nature is the same as ever, so what applied a few thousand years ago, still applies today. God himself also never changes and he says so himself. "I, the Lord, do not change."[2]

Much of what applies to life yesterday, today and tomorrow is dealt with in scripture. You need not wonder what God thinks about the issues that you face today. You need only to read the book.

My children, look into my word for in it are the answers you seek. Seek me in my word for I shall be found there and you shall come to know me by searching my word.

God has made every attempt to make himself and his ways clear to people throughout history. There is no better way to learn about God and understand his character than by reading the Bible, also known simply as his word. He wants to be known and he longs for personal, intimate relationship with each of us. His word tells us what he is really like. From it we can learn to recognize his character.

If we do not take the time to establish a relationship based on the truth of God's character as portrayed in his word, we can easily fall victim to untruths about him.

It is helpful to understand that God has had a lot of bad PR throughout history. As humans with limited knowledge, we tend to believe what we see, and when we don't understand what we see, we make up reasons to try to explain to ourselves why things happen and what they mean. Without adequate and accurate information, we can be off by a wide margin. Since we tend to believe what other people tell us, especially if we have no explanation ourselves, inaccuracy can perpetuate and be disseminated for generations. This is how we end up with beliefs that actually have no truth behind them.

People throughout time have jumped to erroneous conclusions about God when they could not explain or understand the problems that they faced. Rather than seeking truth from God, or searching his word, they came to their own conclusions. This is where superstitions, certain rituals and traditions and false beliefs originate. Then these bewildered folks tell others what they decide is right, and so it goes.

People today are still doing the same thing. If you ever hear people talk about God in a way that puts him in a bad light or blames him for their problems, be aware that they probably don't know God very well. They are jumping to conclusions based on what they can see or what others have said. Most people don't have a good understanding of spiritual matters because our western culture has become so far removed from spiritual awareness, so we are sitting ducks for whatever philosophy or doctrine comes along. This explains the current interest and fascination with angels, spirit guides, channelling, palm reading, other occult practices or the latest mystical craze. As spiritual beings, we are hungry for relationship with God, yet when some don't know how to achieve it, they run after anything that hints of the supernatural. Unless we decide to seek God himself, rather than any phenomenon that gives us goose bumps, we are easy targets for the enemy of our souls.

We need a solid knowledge of God and his ways, so that we can recognize his work in and through us, and also recognize spiritual error. Always start with the assumption that God is good and answer every question or enigma from that perspective.

As we move into a closer relationship with God and begin trying to discern his specific leading for our lives, we must have a basic knowledge of what the character of God is like so that we recognize whose voice we hear. God does not do anything out of character. Everything he does and every way that he relates to you and me lines up with his character. He is not capricious or moody today and laid back or laissez-faire tomorrow. He is steadfast and trustworthy, and by knowing his true character we can learn to recognize his voice instead of following after deceiving spiritual voices.

Just as you must spend time with a new friend to understand what he or she is like, you must also take time to learn what God is like so you can be acquainted with him. He already knows you intimately, which I admit, gives him a definite edge. But this is also an advantage for you because you never have to explain yourself to God. He already knows how you think, why you do what you do, what you want and what you say. His understanding of you and your situation is unlimited.

Let's take a few minutes to look at some of God's characteristics. These are taken directly from scriptures and were included there so that everyone can know him better. As you get to know God on a first person basis, you will understand the following attributes of God's character and discover many others.

God is love

The first thing to understand about God is that he is all about love and has always been all about love. Love is the essential, self-giving, all-encompassing nature of God. He loves and he gives. He loves us so much that the magnitude of his love is incomprehensible. There is little in our world that comes close to comparing to God's love for us except that of a parent toward his or her child. But even the love you have for your children is minor compared to the love God has for you. Spending time just meditating on the fact that God loves you will absolutely change your whole life.

However, if you have trouble accepting that God loves you, just take a look around you. Everything is filled with evidence of his love but we often fail to recognize it. He has created a beautiful world for us to live in that is abundantly filled with goodness. He has provided us with good things like clean, clear water, rich and healthy food, homes to live in, and good friends. If you think that you have created all these things yourself, think again.

Too often we spend our time looking at all that is wrong in our lives, rather than at all the things we have. Once you start looking at all the good in your life, you will see that everything God does for you is over the top. The Bible says that every good and perfect gift comes down from the Father. He lavishes us with his love and care and fills our lives with possibility, opportunity, encouragement and support. He gives and gives and gives. And in loving us, God never gives up the hope of us loving him back.

God is a spirit[4]

We can't see God because he is a spirit. While this does seem to make a developing relationship more challenging, it resembles trying to get to know someone who lives on the other side of the world by using only telephone, email or letters. You can't see her, but she is real and you communicate with her clearly and easily. In the same way, we don't physically see God because he is invisible, but that doesn't make him any less real or approachable. We only have to communicate with him verbally because he is always there.

God does not change

Progress and change happen when God is present and at work, but God, himself, does not change.[5] If he changed, he would not be perfect. If he were not perfect, we would not want him as God. The unpredictable and fickle gods of some of the world's religions are neither personal, all-knowing, all-powerful, nor worthy of our trust. Given the choice between following after the dictates of temperamental gods, or the doctrines of wandering men, I will choose the one true God over all other spiritual beings. God is not different today than he was yesterday. He is the same yesterday, today and always. He won't be changing his mind on you or about you. This makes him eminently trustworthy.

God is completely and utterly powerful

His power knows no limits when it is consistent with his nature, character, and purposes.[6] The only limitations on God's power are limits that God imposed upon himself.[7] So with God, all things are possible.

God does not get tired

It is wonderful to know that God never grows tired or weary[7] and is never unavailable. He will not hang up the phone on you or turn off his computer and go to bed. If you wake in the middle of the night and need to talk, he is there. If you come to him with the same problem again and again, though he wants you to listen to his answer, he will not be too tired to hear you. Look at this verse from the Psalms: "How precious it is, Lord, to realize that you are thinking about me constantly! I can't even count how many times a day your thoughts turn towards me. And when I waken in the morning, you are still thinking of me!" (Psalm 139:17-18, The Living Bible).

God knows everything

There is no knowledge that God does not possess.[8] It is pretty unfathomable for our minds, but he knows everything simultaneously. He knows the thoughts we have and he understands our motives. He knows us inside and out. In fact, he knows us better than we know ourselves.[9] The amazing thing is that while he is looking after me and my needs, he manages to do this for every other person in the world at the same time. God is omniscient.

God is omnipresent

He is not confined to any location, part of space, or time period. He is present everywhere at the same time, all the time.[10] He is the God of the whole earth and the whole universe. The whole universe is filled with His presence. When you send your desires and your wishes out into the universe, you are really putting them into the presence of God. Doesn't that sound better than just sending your wishes out into some great unknown? He pervades and permeates everything. There is nowhere you can go to evade his presence, and nowhere you can hide from him.[11] This means that you are never out of the presence of God no matter what you do or where you go. This is a comforting thought.

God is eternal and forever

This is too much for most of us to comprehend, so don't spend a lot of time sweating over the concept. Accept that God has been around forever and will be around forever. Past, present and future are all known equally to him.[12] His concept of time is way outside the box compared to ours. While we only see time as a string of hours, days, years and centuries, God is able to see and experience time in its entirety, all at once. I know, I don't get it either, but there it is.

God is holy

The word "holy" comes from a root word that means "to separate" and refers to God as separated from or above all other things.[13] Holiness refers to God's moral excellence. The insight that we sometimes find difficult is that because God is holy, he requires holiness and moral excellence from his children. Yet, one of the most extraordinary things about God is that what he demands from us, he also supplies to us. When we accept the gift of his Son, Jesus Christ, by faith, we also receive God's holiness so that we can approach him just as Jesus does.[14] I admit it is a bit mind-boggling, but by choosing to accept this as true, we instantly place ourselves in God's inner circle and become adopted into his family. No matter what your frame of reference may be, he is the perfect father figure because he is perfection itself.

God is righteous

Righteousness is an old-fashioned word that applies to God, but that has taken on a mistaken meaning in our generation. The word "righteous" refers to the affirmation of what is right as opposed to wrong. Even more, it means "in right standing" with God, regardless of performance. Don't confuse this word with self-righteousness. Self-righteousness means to be right in your own eyes, smugly moralistic and intolerant of the opinions of others, whereas righteousness is characterized by uprightness, honesty, integrity, and moral virtue.

Righteousness also refers to God's sense of justice. He knows what is right and what is not, and who is right and who is not. It also refers to God's declaring the believer to be righteous, as though we had never been unrighteous or wrong, because of the sacrificial death of Jesus on our behalf.[15]

God is truth

In fact, God is the personification of truth. He is the benchmark against which all other beliefs, doctrines, ideas, philosophies, and thoughtful meanderings can be measured. Jesus is also the truth. I suspect this is one of those ideas that most of us must choose to accept by faith, because it is simply too abstract to figure out easily. However, there must be a standard of truth in the universe, and my conclusion is that God is it.

God is all-wise

God always knows the best thing to do, at the optimal time, in the choicest way, and for the highest reasons. As you come to know him personally, you will learn to trust in God's wisdom because he always has the most excellent in mind for you. His intentions toward you are always for your best, and in his wisdom, he will lead you to what is the very finest for you no matter what the circumstances.

Even though the Bible gives us excellent guidelines to live by, there will always be some situations in life that are not specifically dealt with. Even if there were rules to govern every area of life, we would not be able to keep them. If you don't believe me, just try making some New Year's resolutions and see if you are still following them by the first week in February. If you read the Old Testament, you will find that the people of that day tried to live by God's laws under their own ability and also failed miserably. You may be familiar with some of these laws recorded in the Ten Commandments. These commandments, put forth by God, are still beneficial for us today because they increase our ability to succeed and experience fulfillment.

God laid down these and other laws to guide the conduct of humans *for our benefit*. People have come to the mistaken conclusion that

God made laws to control us and make our lives miserable. Nothing could be further from the truth. Since God is love and there is nothing but good in him, God could not even suggest anything except that which is for our good.

Now, because Jesus was born to complete and replace the law, there are only two laws that encompass all the previous laws from the Old Testament. These are the only ones we need to remember and follow in order to succeed in pleasing God and living an abundant life. They are as simple as they are perfect:

Love God.

Love others as much as you would love yourself.

Even with only those two simple commands, we often fail. But God honours the person who cares enough about knowing him and about respecting his desires to try daily and he forgives our failings again and again as we continue to seek him.

This gives us a framework for knowing and seeking God. Suffice it to say, we need God's help and thankfully we have a God who cares and is always present to come to our aid when we call on him.

In order to have a relationship with anyone, the most important components are connection and time. If you and I are to become friends, for instance, we need to spend enough time with each other to form a close connection. We must spend time together to get to know each other. You will come to understand what my personality is like and I will get to know you. As we spend time together we learn to know and understand how the other thinks, what our opinions are on different issues, and how we feel about what is important to us.

It is no different with God. You must spend time with him in order to know him. You must read his writings, talk with him about your needs and successes, and sometimes to sit in silence listening for him to speak to you. Having a relationship with an invisible person is much different from a face-to-face connection. It is a little like having a friend in another country who has your phone number but in the beginning, sometimes the phone line is not very clear. As you grow to know the Lord better, the lines of communication become clearer and clearer, but in the beginning it may take some time just to make a connection. So be patient with yourself and don't give up hope. I promise, it gets easier and easier, so that one day soon you will find daily conversation as easy and natural as thinking.

As with an overseas friend, if you never take the time to write or call and your friend never hears or reciprocates, it will not be long before there is no relationship at all. You lose touch and will not have any idea what your friend is up to, and your friend will not be able to share anything with you. Look at these words that the Lord spoke to me one day and I recorded in my journal:

Spend time seeking me. Learn to call on me daily. Stay in me, walk in me, soak yourself in my presence. Then I will pour out my spirit upon you and saturate you with it. For it is only by seeking me that you find me, and knocking that the doors will be opened and by asking that you shall receive.

And it is all in my word. Seek and find. Knock and it will open. Ask and receive answers. Be diligent — the blessing will be great!

How will you spend time with God? What do you have to do in

order to soak in his presence? If you are ready to seek him, there are ways to find him. When you knock, you need to know that you are knocking on the right door. If you are ready to spend the time, make the investment, and open yourself to God's touch, you need to look at how to do that in the most effective way. How do you turn on the light?

As I've already mentioned, you can't get to know God without being willing to spend time with him. If you are ready to find him, you are going to have to make the time to seek. You don't have to go away for days on a retreat, though that is a wonderful idea if you can do it. You don't have to prepare a particular kind of place, or any special equipment, except that you might like to have on hand a journal or notebook, a pen, and a Bible if you have one. If you do not care to write, you don't have to. As I have mentioned earlier, you will have to clear a spot on your schedule at least for a little while, put aside the usual distractions, and use that time only for communion with God.

I recommend that you begin by carving out a space of time during your day when you can be alone and free of interruptions for at least fifteen minutes. If you can take more time, you will receive more from God, but don't be hard on yourself if your life is too full at the moment. The more time you spend alone with God, the more you learn to follow his leading, and the more your life will straighten out. You may find that your priorities become clearer and your commitments lessen as you allow God to reveal his best for you and you follow through on his recommendations. To develop a relationship of open communication between you and God, allow yourself the time and space to relax in his presence. Sometimes the biggest challenge is to stop racing and watching the clock long enough to focus on God.

While God's goal for us is not to make life one long string of beach vacations (would that it were! but we have to wait for heaven for that!), he is also not a tough taskmaster. God has an individualized plan for you that brings into use your most cherished talents and abilities. He will help you order your days so that you are not under constant stress and strain. God is interested in you having peace and joy and abundance, not living at a frantic or hectic pace, suffering pain or sorrow, or living a difficult and miserable existence. While we will look at these issues in depth later in the program, just understand now that God has good things in mind for you.

The problem of having or making the time to spend with God is not primarily one of time management, though it may appear that way at first glance. We all have busy lives to the degree that we fill them up with things that we want to do, or feel that we have to do.

Finding time to be alone with God is a priority issue. We can all reschedule our lives to fit something different in *if we are convinced of the importance or urgency of it.* If you don't believe me, just think of the last time you had a sick child or a project deadline at work. Suddenly, priorities fall into a different line, and the urgent or essential rises to the top of your list while the less important drop to the bottom, or even right off the list entirely. When this happens, everything besides the urgent takes on less importance by comparison.

Take a look at your daily agenda and mark in time to be alone with God. Once you decide to make spending time with God a priority in your life, you will have to make a firm commitment to follow through. You can be sure that there will suddenly come all sorts of minutiae that interfere with your quiet time. That's because the enemy of your soul wants to prevent you from knowing, trusting, and loving God. The more distractions he can throw in your path the more likely you are to give up. My advice is, don't give him the satisfaction!

Once you decide to be on God's team, it is up to you to make the decision stick, so don't waffle and don't look back. God will be alongside to help you and guide you, but you must exert some effort too. He says he is a rewarder of those who *diligently* seek him, and oh, those rewards are sweet.

[2]Malachi 3:6

[3] Psalms 46:1

[4] John 4:24

[5] Hebrews 1:12

[6] Genesis 17:1, 18:14

[7] Isaiah 40:28

[8] Isaiah 40:27-31

[9] Job 38:39; Rom 11:33-36

[10]Job 37:16; Ps 147:5, and Heb 3:13

[11] Ps 139:7-12

[12] Genesis 18:25

[13] 2 Peter 3:8; Rev 1:8

[14] Isaiah 6:1-3

[15] Ephesians 4:24

[16] Romans 1:16-17, 3:24-26

Journal

In this chapter we talk about spending the time to get to know God better and to begin to develop a close one-on-one relationship with him. There are times in all our lives when we feel that we are 'doing life' all alone. Tell about a time when you have felt this way.

God is interested in every detail of our lives. In this chapter, I describe an experience I had buying shoes and how God helped me to choose the right pair. Can you think of a time when you asked for God's help in making decisions and things worked out well? Tell about that. At the time did you recognize that God was working on your behalf?

Although nothing could be further from the truth, many people believe that God only thinks about them when he is angry. In fact, God thinks about you all the time and with good thoughts to help you live a better, happier life. If you have trouble with this concept, explore where and how it may have begun.

Do you have trouble believing that God is intensely interested in your life? He plays no favourites and loves you as much as he does any of the world's great leaders or mystics. Here is an exercise to help you believe this. Write down the names of several people whom you esteem highly, either who are living now or are historical figures then say or write the phrase, "God loves me as much as he loves..." and fill in the blank with each of those names.

For example you could say, "God loves me as much as he loves Mother Teresa." "God loves me as much as he loves the Pope." As you meditate on this truth, you will find that your self-esteem will soar as you become convinced that you are highly esteemed by God.

Have you ever been involved in a tragedy and asked God for comfort? If not, why not? If you did turn to God, how did you sense his comfort and presence?

God uses many methods to speak to his children, such as dreams, visions, or thoughts in our conscious minds. Have you ever had the experience of one of these and known that you had received a message from God? Write about that experience.

One of the most obvious methods that God uses to communicate with us is through his written word, the Bible. If you do not yet have one, I urge you to get one as soon as you can and begin reading it. Why do you suppose that God had people through the ages create such a book? As you read, can you see the character of God? List some of the great qualities now.

I mention above that throughout history God has gotten a bad reputation from people who have little understanding of him and his ways. Can you think of instances in your own life when people have blamed God when bad things happened, or implied that God is not on your side?

If you believe that God is not totally on your side, it will be difficult to trust him with your problems and your cares. It is vitally important to eradicate any false beliefs about the nature of God. To do that we must find out what he is really like by reading his word, talking with him, and replacing wrong beliefs with correct ones. Meditating on truths about God will help you change your thinking. Even something as simple as repeating that God is good and that he loves you completely will replace wrong thinking with truth. What other ways can you use to change how you view God so that it is one hundred percent positive?

In this chapter we discuss the different attributes of God that are so important to know, beginning with, God is love. Read over the description of how God shows his love to you and meditate on it. As you do, you may want to write down your thoughts on the subject, too.

Even though God is a Spirit, we can still develop a warm and close relationship with him. Sometimes it helps to see God's attributes in others to remind us of how God feels about us. If you can think of someone in your life who has been good, kind of loving toward you, this is a demonstration of how God will treat you too. Write about some of those people or experiences.

Knowing that God does not change is a great comfort and demonstrates his trustworthiness. He will not be changing his mind about how much he loves you or how much he wants to help you improve your life. Write about how this knowledge impacts your life.

I used to think that I was bothering God with issues in my life that I should be able to handle myself. Since others might have bigger, more important problems to take up God's time, I thought he would not be interested in my daily stuff. I was wrong, and I am so glad I learned to connect with God about everything. Have you experienced similar feelings and how will you change now that you know he is interested in everything?

God is everywhere at once and knows everything. Knowing that we cannot hide anything from him even if we wanted to takes away any reason not to be completely open with him. And because he in infinitely kind, we can trust him with everything. How does this make you feel?

Holiness is a concept that is sometimes difficult to grasp, but it has to do with total excellence in all things, which describes God. By accepting Jesus into our own lives God's holiness also becomes ours. How does this knowledge change how you see yourself and God?

Jesus told us that there are only two instructions that we must now live by, love God and love others as much as you would love yourself. Can you see that by this directive, you must also love yourself if you are to love others? Is it easier to love yourself, knowing that God loves you so completely? How does that feel?

Spending time alone with God is vital to creating a close relationship. What times are there in your day when you can carve out this alone time? Why not include those times in your calendar now and make it easier to show up for your daily appointments with God?

Beginning a journal will help you to record your experiences and feelings as you spend time with God. Write down your feelings and questions, and what you believe God is saying to your or bringing to your mind as you talk with him. Enjoy your times with him and you will look forward to those times more and more. What questions might you ask God right now?

FOUR
The Gentle Voice

Some years ago God placed an incredible dream in my heart and mind. I can't identify a time or a day when it began, and at first it was more like an idea that occurred to me rather than a life-changing epiphany. I gave it a little thought, then forgot about it. Another day, the idea occurred to me again, long enough for me to give it some more thought. After a while, since the idea kept popping into my head, I began to apply a little imagination to it before letting it go again. Over the course of some months, the seed of the idea sprouted tiny roots and pushed up a miniature leaf or two.

The dream that God had planted in the soil of my soul was to live in France. It came to me as a simple desire that had perhaps lain dormant in my subconscious for some time, but when the time was ripe, it began to grow. As time went on, I allowed myself to imagine briefly my little family living in France. Visions of buying bright-coloured vegetables and exotic foods at the outdoor markets, smelling the aroma of fresh-baked croissants in a village boulangerie, strolling along poppy-lined country lanes, and driving down narrow roads between vineyards began to tantalize me. It didn't take long until the idea of taking my family to live in France changed from a wishful, yet impossible, dream to seeming quite plausible and I actively entertained the concept of moving there, finding income, and setting up a home.

At the time it all began, I had two young children, one of whom was already attending elementary school, and a husband who had a job that he expected to stay at until retirement, or at least for many more years. I owned a small business in the beauty industry that allowed me to be at home with my children and make a decent part-time income. My older daughter was happy in her school which was an easy walk from our house and from which she could come home for lunch each day. She was involved in school programs and extra-curricular activities. My youngest would soon be joining her in school, too.

The prospect of selling our home, storing our furniture and vehicles, folding my business, and my husband resigning from his secure job and leaving the country were the furthest things from the minds of my family members. So, over and over, I dismissed the idea as too far-fetched. It made no sense. I now know that often dreams from God only make sense in retrospect. If they were easy to achieve, they wouldn't be dreams.

I had studied the French language in high school as have most other students in Canada. I have an affinity for languages and always loved French. I had travelled briefly in France some years before and enjoyed my experiences there, so the desire to live in France didn't come totally out of the blue.

However, the prospect of only another visit to the country was not enough. A simple holiday abroad just didn't cut it. God had begun to nudge me in the direction he wanted me to go. He had placed the desire in me not just to visit France but to go and actually live there. Living in a foreign country is vastly different from visiting one. Travelling and setting up home with two children and a bag of home-schooling materials for two different grades presents many special challenges.

The requirement to find work in an unfamiliar language and in a country with radically different requirements and laws to those of your homeland can be downright scary.

Because my husband was born in Britain and holds a British passport, he had the advantage of being able to work legally in the EC countries. Now you must understand, none of us had any family connection to France, nor did we have any particular reason to go. As the desire to live in France began to take root, I started searching for possible options for us for a work situation and a place to live. Over the course of a couple of years, the desire to live in France had become the driving passion of my life. I researched options, saved money for airfares and began to make plans. I scoured my local library for books about contemporary France, the economy, jobs and opportunities, and different regions and housing possibilities. This was happening in the late 1980s, in the days prior to internet access so researching was more difficult and time-consuming than it is now. The more I thought about going, the more I couldn't stop thinking about it. The more I imagined how it could work out, the more ideas I got on how to make it work.

During this time, I spent a lot of time talking to God about moving to France. Though at first it didn't cross my mind that this plan came from God, I had finally grasped that this crazy dream was his idea, but knew that I had to do my part to bring the fulfillment. I knew that I had to be prepared to move in order for God's plan to work. I made prayer dates with my cousins and my aunt who lived in the same city and who were willing to support me and believe in my dream. We spent many hours seeking God for direction and for help.

I also began to talk to my children about living in France. Children make the best cheering section. They believe what you tell them and simply assume that because you've said it, then it must be true, therefore, it will happen just as you've said. Their incredible faith is a good example for the rest of us of how to believe. So when I talked to my children about moving to France, they automatically took it that one day we would be doing just that.

I didn't know why God gave me such an absurd desire. But I know that often God places dreams in our hearts to lead us in the direction he wants us to take. Had I been able to see the end from the beginning, it may have been easier, or it may not have. In any case, I did not know why this desire to live in France began to grow within me; I just knew that it did.

While all this dreaming and planning was taking place, my husband kept going to work and living his life with the expectation that nothing was going to change. I had talked to him about living in France but he made it clear that he had no intention of moving there. In fact, I think he viewed the whole idea as just another of his wife's hare-brained schemes that, if ignored, would soon fade away, requiring no effort or response from him. He had not, however, reckoned on the Holy Spirit.

When God wants to get your attention, he uses means that will guarantee the right response from you - your desires. As you put yourself into the hands of God, expecting and trusting that what he wants for you is what is best for you, you allow God to begin to direct your steps. If you want God to lead you, then he will lead you. Be assured, he will find ways to get his ideas across to you whether you think you can hear his voice or not. God has a great imagination, and the wisdom of the universe, so he has countless methods at his disposal. And he knows exactly what works for you.

This is what happened to me. I had set my intention to be led by the Holy Spirit. This was a lifestyle decision, a definite choice. Though I didn't really know how to be led by the Spirit, I just knew that I wanted to be and that I wanted whatever God considered his best for me. So he made it easy for me to know what he wanted me to do. He placed a desire in my heart and mind that, as it grew, caused me to long for what he wanted to happen. What began as a single thought, over time expanded to become a burning, unrelenting desire, a desire that had to have fulfillment in order for me to live a peaceful life.

God will never give you a dream and leave you high and dry without helping you to bring it to pass. As you will see, this dream that he gave me came to pass and changed my life. You see, God knows you better than anyone does. He knows your history, your family's history, your thoughts, your feelings, your opinions, your good personality traits and your not-so-pretty ones. He understands why you do what you do and how you can change. He knows how you are made, what makes you happy and what troubles you. Nothing you do surprises God. He is unshockable and unshakable.

When we choose to submit to the desires and wishes of God, we make the most astounding decision of our lives. Suddenly, we realize that we no longer have to go it alone. When we ask for God's help, we have the assurance that he will take whatever part of us that we are willing to give him and make it better.

God has given us each a free will. It wasn't even our own idea to have free will; it was his idea. He is so in love with us that he had to give us a free will in order to be assured that our allegiance to him would be entirely voluntary. After all, what joy is there in forcing someone to love you or spend time with you?

God is interested in absolutely every aspect of our lives. He cares about the tiniest things. He is happy when we are happy, and he comforts us when we are troubled or sad. God is infinitely tenderhearted toward us. God loves us with an everlasting love. He loved each of us long before we were born and will continue to love us long after we have left this world. I am sure you would agree that this love is a truly great love and is also a great consolation.

As I have sought God through the years, I have come to know and understand God's great love, even though it is still sometimes difficult to appreciate the magnitude of it. We tend to see things in terms we already understand, yet God's terms are so much loftier that ours that sometimes it's easier just to take him at his word. To me, he has proven himself to be eminently trustworthy, so I continue to choose to believe what he says. That way I place myself in a position to experience his leading. You will find that as you place your trust in God, he will prove himself to be the most reliable guide and helper that you will ever know.

God leads us in a myriad of ways. The Bible describes many where God spoke directly to individuals. Sometimes he spoke through an angel, or through dreams, and once even used a donkey! (I don't know about you, but if a donkey began to talk to me, I would stop and listen!) Though I know that God still sometimes uses unusual means of communications when he sees fit, I believe for the most part he speaks to each of us individually in a variety of easily recognizable ways.

When God began to speak to me about moving to France, it began as a tiny thought, a passing wish. When I didn't immediately jump at it, he brought it up again and again until I turned my thoughts in his direction. I sometimes wonder if he had assigned an angel just to follow me around and keep whispering in my ear about living in France.

The voices of God the Father, the Holy Spirit, and of Jesus are sometimes perceived as three different voices, and sometimes just one voice. I tend to think of them all as the Lord, since when you have given Jesus governing authority in your life, he is the Lord of your life. He is also your advocate with God. The Holy Spirit is your comforter. It is not important at this time to try to discern whose voice you are hearing, so don't spend any time puzzling about that right now.

God spoke to me in ways that were very natural and understandable - a thought, a wish, an idea, a consideration. Then when I mentioned my dream to my friends and confidants, I believe that he used them to encourage me to pursue the plan of living in France.

The important thing to know is that the voice of God is almost always a gentle voice. God is never pushy, loud or rude. In the same way that you would speak gently to a young child or a lover in a tender moment, God speaks to you. I am not saying that he never gives definite words or firm instructions, or that he never reminds you or urges you to follow his directions, just that he does not speak without love in his voice. Occasionally, God must speak firmly or insistently to get your attention, or chastise you in the manner of a loving dad, but when your heart is tuned to hear God's voice, he does not need to shout. Your soul will hear a gentle voice. But first you must turn down the noise around you.

Most people's lives today are characterized by busyness, rushing, and stress. Most of us are familiar with spending long days at work, in meetings, running children to school and activities, social engagements, plus various commitments and special events. Mine was no exception. Responsibilities and obligations more than fill the hours of the day and most of us fall into bed exhausted at night. Sometimes I wonder if some of us over-fill our days so that we don't have time to look into our own hearts and feel the pain and emptiness that we carry around. It does not have to be this way.

As the desire to live in France grew, I began to take time to give it my attention. I spent time alone with God, talking with him and listening for his words of assurance that I was on the right track and that this dream came from him. I also began to make plans for how we could accomplish such a venture, seeking God's guidance frequently.

Gradually, as my wish to move to France turned into desire, and the desire produced plans, the plans initiated the actions. God smoothed out the wrinkles. Difficulties like an unwilling husband, finding satisfactory solutions for schooling, moving and storing our belongings, and selling our house were handled one by one. When push came to shove, I knew I could not give up my dream of living in France, so the Holy Spirit spoke to my husband's heart. He simply changed his mind and agreed to go along with it. This demonstrated a great act of courage on his part, and I am forever grateful for this man's willingness to believe in my dream and support me in bringing it to pass.

Once we arrived in Europe a whole new set of challenges presented themselves and we tackled them with God's help, again one by one. We found a position working as caretakers for a couple who owned an eighteenth-century estate in Provence. In many ways this situation was beyond our wildest dreams and the timing of our arrival was perfect. Our sojourn in Europe and our experiences living in France turned out to be the grand adventure of all our lives. Yet it never would have happened if I hadn't heard those initial whispers from God and decided to listen.

In the same way that I did, I recommend that you begin including "God time" in your daily calendar. This may mean getting up earlier than you are used to, staying up a little later, or setting aside time in your day when you can get away from the noise and the rush, away from all of the other demands that vie for your attention and be alone with God. In order to learn to hear God's voice, you have to make this a priority. Your future peace and happiness depend on it.

Look around and find a place where you can be free from interruption or intrusion. This will mean walking away from your computer and turning off your cell phone or palm device. It will mean finding a place where no one will talk to you, request anything from you, or make noise around you. If you live in a busy household, it may be as simple as closing your bedroom door with a "Do Not Disturb" sign hanging from the doorknob, or retreating to the bathroom and running the bath. You don't even have to get in the bath if you don't want to, though I'm sure you would find that might help to relax you and focus your mind.

Perhaps you have a cozy corner where you can curl up in a chair. Maybe your place of solitude is on a beach, on a walk through a park, or in your parked car. The important thing is that you find a place where you can be alone. If you have a Bible, I suggest you take it along since reading it helps you to focus on the things of the Spirit. You don't have to create a lot of fanfare around your times with God. Just tell the people you live with that you would like a little time alone, then go into another room and close the door, leaving instructions that you don't want to be disturbed.

As you turn to God in your mind, try to put aside any thoughts and worries that obstruct your mental view of Jesus. When I want to get really close to God and need to hear his voice, I begin by making a command out loud, that all voices except the voice of God, Jesus, or the Holy Spirit be silenced. I always follow the command with the phrase, "in the name of Jesus," since Jesus said that whatever we ask in his name, he would see that it be done. As a believer in Jesus, you have the authority to use his name in this manner.

Since your mind is probably a very busy place, it is also a good idea figuratively to put aside all thoughts, plans, pre-occupations or ideas that would distract you from focusing on God. I do this by imagining that whatever comes to mind which is not about God be placed onto a tablecloth beside me. Once all those interruptions have come up, I gather up the corners of the tablecloth so it makes a big bundle, and mentally hand it all over to God. This allows me to concentrate on him alone, while letting him look after my stuff for me.

In order to hear a soft voice, you must be in a quiet place, both in your surroundings and in your mind. The more time you spend with God, the more you will learn how to find that quiet place inside where the Spirit speaks to you. As your own spirit grows more and more ac-customed to the sound of God's voice, you will find that you can have ongoing internal conversations regardless of your surroundings. But even then, your soul needs a break and your quiet time with God is invaluable.

As you grow to know God more and more, and turn to him for direction in your life, he will speak into your spirit and guide you through your thoughts. This is what he did with me regarding moving to France. He whispered his desire into my spirit and his thoughts became my thoughts.

It is so sweet to me when you come just to be close to me. How I long for your company. It bothers me that you see being with me as work. Clearly, you have the wrong impression. For being with me is rest; it is joy; it is freedom. Being in my presence is a break from the work of life.

When you take the time to be alone with me, that is when I can restore your soul. You can lay your head upon my shoulder and close your eyes and I will comfort you. I lift the cares of the world from your shoulders, never to place them back on you. The cares that you carry are what you have picked up. They are not cares I have placed upon you.

What I ask of you is easy and the burdens I ask you to carry are light. I ask little of you, only your devotion and faith. I ask only that you be my friend and do my will.

In me there is continual joy. This is the place of the joy of the Lord. It is by being continually in my presence. We are not separate except if you distance yourself from me. I am with you always as I promised. Your awareness of my continual presence will bring forth the joy of the Lord in you.

Know that you are continually in the presence of joy; love and good cheer flow out of me and surround you perpetually. There is no way you can avoid it if you stay close to me. When you distance yourself from me in fear, you move out of my circle of joy. When you sense a lack of joy in your life, that is a sure sign that you are drifting away from me.

The way to stay close to me is to think of me first in everything, then talk to me. We can be in constant communication.

For example, if you go out for the day with a friend, you are in continual communication. You wander through the stores together commenting on this and that, have lunch, drive here or there and the conversation flows continually. It is the same with spending the day with me. Everywhere we go and in whatever we do, the conversation never stops.

The difference is that I am the Lord of the Universe and I am your Lord and what you ask of me, I will do, and have the ability to do. That makes our relationship so much greater than a person-to-person friendship. I bring with me the power to change things at your request. So as we converse during our day, ask me for whatever you require and it will be done for you. Make your day a constant prayer with me for that is our conversation.

Remember that I am the first one you should talk to about your problems. Not only am I the nearest one you can talk to but I am the only one who can effect change in you, in others, in circumstances, in the world.

This is the life of continual, total joy. It is one totally enveloped, submerged, soaked, and lost in me.

The gentle Holy Spirit will accompany you as you go through your day. All you have to do is talk to him and expect to hear him talk to you. The more you do this, it will become easier and easier to hear him.

Let me give you an example. I live in a small town and work in my home office. I try to begin every day with some quiet time with God. Sometime between when I rise and before I turn on my computer to connect with the rest of the world, I go into the room that used to be my daughter's bedroom before she moved away from home. My husband and I now use it as a guest room, where we have a fold-down futon, a computer space for him, and a sewing corner for me. The view from the window of this room looks out past my honeysuckle vine and the forsythia bush, past the next-door neighbour's house to a spectacular mountain peak and forest-covered mountains reaching out in a panorama as far as I can see. It faces east, so when the sky is cloudless, I often see the sun rise over the mountain range, staining the sky pink and warming the room with its rays upon my feet. I keep my Bible and usually several other books on the futon sofa where I sit in the morning to read and talk to God.

These times are very precious to me. Now that my children have grown and gone, and my husband goes off to work, the house is mine alone. It sounds lovely, I know, and it is. But keep in mind that I run a business from the rooms next door and the demands of the various projects in my life call constantly.

Frequently, I travel on business, sometimes only as far as the next big town, sometimes all day in the city, a two-hour drive from my home, or flying to conferences and trade shows around the continent.

I travel alone most of the time, but I know that I am never alone. Jesus said he would never leave me nor forsake me, so I can expect his presence with me wherever I go.

I am a creative person, so my mind is usually on many thoughts or ideas at once. I tend to create projects in my mind before anything ends up on paper either in the form of writing or artwork, and I find that I work best when I can mull ideas over for a while before I begin to work on new endeavours. Needless to say, this makes me a little absent-minded!

When I travel, I rely heavily on the direction of the Holy Spirit. I tend to forget which boarding area I am supposed to go to even though I may have just read it a few minutes before. I get distracted by people passing by me, or the scents from the shop selling bath products, or by the title of a new book in the airport bookstore. Out of necessity, I must stay in constant conversation with God. He acts as my guide, my reminder, my direction finder and my caretaker.

As I move through airports and strange cities, I ask him to show me where I need to go and remind me when I must be at my departure gate. When I drive I ask for his help in getting where I need to be on time. I need him to show me what streets to take and where to turn. It is hard to read a map while you are driving in a strange city! I even ask for good parking spots.

Is it easy to hear and follow God? As you will discover for yourself, the answer is yes and no. However, the main secret to communication with God is to expect an answer. He knows your questions before you ask them and he knows the desires of your heart. He also has every answer to every question you could ever have. But he is waiting for you to ask, break the ice and start the dialogue. His gentle voice will lead you and help you once you expect him to answer when you drop in for a talk.

Journal

In this chapter I relate the story of how God gave me the dream of living in France. Though we don't always understand why God leads us down certain paths, we can always know that the results will be good and for our ultimate good. God often places desires in our hearts for what he wants us to do. Have you ever had the experience of feeling led or called by to follow a certain path or direction in your life? Tell about that. How did you sense it was God speaking to you?

I believe that one of the reasons that God led me so clearly was that I had set my intention to be led by the Spirit. If you have never done so, I encourage you to make the same decision for yourself. Let me assure you again that his plan is only for your benefit. This does not mean that everything in life will be rosy from now on, rather that you have a supernatural helper to assist and guide you through your days. How do you feel about that?

The Holy Spirit leads us with a gentle voice, never condemning, never harsh. Those voices "in your head" may be God talking to you through your spirit; may be your own mind, or may be the enemy accusing you. If what you hear is not encouraging, loving or kind, you can be sure that you are not hearing God speak to you. Now, find a quiet place where you can be free from distractions and ask God to speak to you. You may have a question or a problem that you would like his help with. Simply ask him what you want and then sit quietly and listen. Usually what happens is a thought or thoughts will come to you. Weigh these carefully. Does this answer sound loving, kind, supportive and good? If it does, then you can trust that was God speaking to you. If it does not, then tell those other voices to be silent and try again. Write about your experience here.

When God began speaking to me about moving to France, it started as a single thought, then grew to become much more. Do you have wishes, desires or goals that began small yet have grown to become more insistent of your attention? Describe how that has happened for you.

Have you ever had the experience of sensing a strong leading to do something, go somewhere or contact someone? Were you aware that the source of this leading may have been God? Describe what that was like for you.

When God wants to lead you, he often uses your own wishes, passions or desires to encourage you to follow him. Can you think of a time that you were filled with a wish or desire to do something or go somewhere that you did or did not recognize as God's direction?

When we choose to submit to the desires and wishes of God, he comes along side us to help us in our pursuits. If you have a desire or dream that you feel comes from God, you can ask him to help you in pursuit of that aspiration. Tell about ways that you can think of to access God's help in achieving your dreams.

One way that you can grow in your understanding of how God speaks to you is to simply ask him to. As you go through your day, talk to God and see what he says to you. When you speak to him, you can expect an answer or a conversation. Give this a try and write about how this worked for you.

In this chapter, I tell about how I deal with mental interruptions to my quiet time with God by imagining that I take each of those interrupting thoughts and place them on a tablecloth near me, then gather up the corners of the cloth and hand the bundle to God to look after for me. What ways can you think of to clear your mind of mental interruptions so you can concentrate on God?

God is the Lord of the universe. He has the ability to do anything, but that does not mean he will. God is constrained by our faith and his wisdom. As we develop in faith and the Spirit and God's wisdom is imparted to us, our choices conform more and more to his choices for us. What are your thoughts on this?

Since God is interested in every detail of your life, you can learn to entrust more of your day-to-day problems and issues to him. He does not require more of us than we are able to do. Write down all the ways you can think of that you can seek God's help throughout your day.

FIVE
What to Avoid

When I was a teenager in high school one of my older cousins decided to get married. Since I had spent many years learning to play the piano, Linda asked me to provide the musical accompaniment for her wedding ceremony. The only problem was that the church where the ceremony was to take place did not have a piano; it had only an organ.

Though they have some similarities, pianos and organs have enough differences that I knew I had to learn to play the organ before I could do a good job at the wedding. Since my cousin lived quite a distance away from me, I made an arrangement with a local church to use their organ during the week so I could practice the music for the wedding.

One afternoon as I was deep in practice I looked up and noticed that the sky had clouded over ominously and the wind had picked up. Tree branches outside the church windows whipped and swayed in the increasing gusts. A downpour could not be far behind. Since my drive home to the farm followed only dirt roads, and I knew that with very little rain the surfaces of those roads became either slick as grease or as thick and sticky as bread dough, I needed to leave immediately to beat the storm.

I hurriedly locked up the church and ran for my car, leapt behind the wheel and sped away. I drove fast and for part of the ten-mile drive the road was dry, but then the storm broke. Torrents of rain fell. I turned my wipers on high but the rain splattered my windshield faster than the wipers could slap it away. I knew from driving with my dad that the only way to stay on these roads when they are wet was to keep moving fast. I pressed on the gas pedal and blasted through the stretch of road where the soil is thick, black and becomes like glue under your wheels. The mud splattering the underside of the car sounded like a continuous volley of machine gun rounds.

Then I crested the hill where the type of soil abruptly changes. On this stretch of the road for more than a mile, the surface when wet is more slippery than oil on glass. I sped on, knowing that one slip of the wheel would land me in the ditch. In the low stretches, these ditches were still filled with water from the spring run-off. My hands gripped the steering wheel as I barrelled along.

Then it happened. My tire caught the edge of a rut. The car swerved. I corrected, a little too much. Then the back tires caught another rut. The car fishtailed, spun sideways and headed straight for the ditch, lurching to a thudding stop nose down in the sodden grass and weeds.

I was so shocked and startled by my sudden landing that I burst into tears. I knew from the angle of the car and the state of the road that I would never be able to back out. Though I was only a couple of miles from home, it was still raining hard and had turned cold. Since I was dressed in light summer clothes and sandals, I did not relish a "stroll" in this weather. In a few moments, I dried my tears and tried to think of a solution to my problem.

When I lifted my head from where I'd leaned it on the steering wheel I noticed a tractor coming toward me across the field. The weather had stopped him from working the ground. In a few minutes he pulled out of the field and onto the road, drove up behind my car and stopped. The farmer got out, looked over my situation, attached a chain to the car and hauled it and me out of the ditch. By this time the squall was nearly over, so I put my car in gear and drove gratefully on home, this time at a somewhat more moderate pace.

If you want to continue down the road to a beautiful relationship with your God, there are certain things you need to avoid. Just as I needed to avoid the ditches on my way home in the rainstorm, we need to avoid wandering or slipping off the road when it comes to hearing God's voice.

Don't be superficial.

Religious form and prescribed formal behaviour are unnecessary and can even be detrimental to an open communication with God. Trying to be something you are not is hard work, and pointless any-way. God knows exactly who you are and what you are like, so faking anything, pretending holiness, putting up a false front or any other form of artifice is a waste of time. God sees through it all. God created you to be you because that's how he loves you to be.

You do not have to act a certain way, except with respect, and you do not have to perform any rituals for God to want to spend time with you. You are okay just as you are and when you approach God, make it honestly and authentically. This makes God happy.

Many people believe that the way they have lived in the past now prevents or disqualifies them from seeking God. They feel that their record is simply too besmirched for God to want to have anything to do with them. Knowing that you have broken the law, done drugs, lied, stolen, cheated, or just been a miserable person will not prejudice God against you. What comes between you and God is not so much the deeds of your past but not admitting and being freed from them, so be real and be prepared to change. You can have no cleansing from your past mistakes until you are willing to acknowledge that you've blown it and seek Jesus' mercy and clemency.

Lay aside your own agenda.

Second, try not to come to God with only your own agenda in mind. God does not seem to regard time the same way we do, so what we think will be good timing to accomplish our goals may be a complete mismatch with what God has in mind. He is never in a hurry, yet is always on time.

I am the first to admit that I have often come to God with my own agenda. When I was praying, planning, and preparing to go live in France, I had a definite idea when the move should take place. I was pretty clear about what I thought would work well for our family. I chose a date that I wanted to be ready to go by, when we should fly to Europe, and had created my plan of how everything should work out. I presented my agenda to God with the full expectation that he would be ready to run with it, making it all supernaturally come to pass just as I'd planned. I expected everything to fall into place right on schedule. To my amazement and confusion, it did not.

As my proposed departure date drew near, I became more and more aware that things were not turning out the way I had planned. My husband, for instance, was nowhere near making any decision to move to France. Though his co-operation in my plan was a major piece of the puzzle, he persistently believed that he would wake up one morning and I would have gotten over all my goofy ideas about moving overseas. I had also made plans regarding how our house would sell, including when and for how much. That didn't happen on my schedule either.

In fact, as my appointed day came and went and it seemed like we were not one step closer to moving to Europe, my optimism and enthusiasm came crashing down. I knew God had given me the dream of living in France, yet it seemed like after that he'd just gotten up and walked off, leaving me holding the bag. For a long time it seemed like my cherished dream might never become reality at all. I was disappointed and bewildered.

I am not suggesting that you not make plans. That would be foolhardy and unproductive, not to mention unlike God's ways. But my experience taught me a valuable lesson. God does not dance to my tune.

Though God longs to give us the desires of our hearts, he views our lives from a vantage point that we can never have. What I didn't know (and God did) was that the best time to go to France was not my due date. I discovered that there were things I desperately needed to learn that would set me free in many areas of my life, and I needed to know them in order to receive what he had for me regarding my France dreams. He wanted to change my thinking on certain issues before I could benefit from all that he had in store for me in the European experience. He also had to help my husband understand some things for him to be able to benefit from this experience. What we didn't know was that God was busy, setting things up to work for our optimal good on many fronts. If he had permitted us to move on my schedule, nothing would have turned out like it did. I am still immensely thankful that it happened God's way, not mine.

Please note that I am also not implying that you should not be clear about your requests when you talk to God. I believe it is very important to know what you want and be definite about it. But like any child, we don't always get what we want, just when we want it. And like any good parent, God does know what's best for us. But when you are convinced that what you want is God's will for you, don't let anything stop you from standing firm. Even if things don't turn out exactly as you imagine, don't give up believing and moving toward your goal. God is behind you every step of the way; he may just have better plans for working out the best results. In fact, my experience has been that God's answer is usually much more and much better than what you asked for in the first place.

Avoid moving forward without directions.

People frequently get a sense of direction from God and then run with it without first checking what to do next. Often we are so anxious for divine direction, that rather than spend time getting clear instructions about what God wants us to do, we hear God tell us one thing, then take off in pursuit of it before finding out if there is more we need to know.

When the angel of the Lord visited Jesus' mother Mary to announce to her that she was to give birth to the Son of God, you can imagine that she may have been somewhat taken aback. First of all, she could have run out of that room screaming in fright at having seen an apparition. But she didn't. Evidently, either she was accustomed to seeing and conversing with angels, or he made such an impression on her that she was stunned into silence.

Alternately, she might have taken the news and told all her girlfriends and the neighbourhood gossips. After all, giving birth to the Messiah could be considered quite a coup. Or she could have taken to her bed and feigned a fever, flatly refusing to have anything to do with such a cockamamie plan. She might even have insisted that Joseph marry her that instant to cover it up her pregnancy. But she didn't.

The biblical account says that she "pondered all these things in her heart." Mary was wise beyond her years, and no doubt was raised to have great respect and reverence for God. She believed the angel and submitted to God's bidding. Then she kept her mouth shut and waited for God to tell her what would happen next and what she should do. We can learn a lot from this young woman's example.

I come from a family of doers (which is probably why we were called the Dewars – and it is pronounced the same way). Only a couple of generations back they were pioneers and homesteaders, determined and self-reliant people. I learned from a young age, that if you want something done, you have to get up and do it yourself. If things are not the way you like them, then you have the power and ability to change them. These are good things to learn and I'm grateful for the can-do attitude that my family instilled in me. However, there have been times when this method of living has gotten in the way of God working in my life. I usually have no trouble hearing God speak and am willing (sometimes after a little persuasion) to obey what God has asked me to do. But very often, rather than taking God's instructions and asking him how he would like me accomplish his directives, I instead just start "doing."

Fortunately, I've learned over the years that doing things this way is doing things the hard way. God will not only lead you in what he has for you to do, but he will help you en route. Consulting with God regularly will save you a lot of time and trouble.

Don't try to do it on your own.

Avoid trying to accomplish God's will on your own, with your own strength or your own plans. Working with God is a joint venture, not a delegation. When you partner with God for your life, remember that the arrangement involves every area of your life, not just those areas where you ask for or need help. God wants everything in your life to be brand new and better, so his plans for you usually include what is best in other spheres, too, and sometimes includes people close to you as well. When you decide to move off after your dreams without waiting for God's direction, you can actually interfere with God's plans to give you the desires of your heart. After all, if you are convinced that you can carry out his instructions on your own, and without his help, why should he intervene?

I know from experience that many times I sensed God's direction in my life and then proceeded to try to figure out on my own how to make everything work. Waiting and trusting can be frustrating, even nerve-wracking sometimes, but there are many instances in my life where I would have saved myself a ton of time and money by not taking off to do my own thing with little more than an inspiring thought.

Stay close to me. Continually consult me. Try to get into the habit of talking to me about everything. As you get further from me, it becomes more difficult to hear my voice so stay close to me always. Talk to me about everything and I will be there beside you to help in everything. You will need my continual support for the work you are doing and are about to do. Stay in close communion with me or you will begin working under your own strength and effort. You don't want that to happen because not only will your energy be depleted rapidly but, your work will not meet with nearly the degree of success as if you use my power.

Avoid listening to evil spirits.

As you learn to be led by the Spirit, you will become more and more aware of the world of the spirits. Yes, there are many spirits in the atmosphere that we don't see, but are real nonetheless. There are believers who have been given the spiritual gift that allows them to discern different spirits, both angelic and demonic, and we will look at that more in depth later. However, most of us do not have the gift of actually seeing into the spirit world. That is why it is so important to take the time to learn and study about spiritual matters. Again, I use the Bible as my reference. If you study the ministry of Jesus, you will see that he encountered many instances of evil spirits at work in people's lives. Since spirits do not die, we can assume that if they were giving folks trouble in Jesus' day, they are still causing disorder, disruption, and mayhem wherever they can get away with it today.

I don't advocate spending a lot of time focusing on devils and evil spirits because it's unprofitable and places too much attention on the negative. I would much rather spend my time getting to know God.

The closer I get to God the more I understand the spirit world. God will alert me to those times when evil spirits are trying to have their way in my life. By studying God's word, I increase my understanding of the various problems that are caused by evil spirits. The easiest way to understand the work of evil spirits in the world today is to remember that Satan's mandate is to steal, kill and destroy. If you are experiencing anything related to these results, then you can be pretty sure there are devils at work.

That doesn't mean that you start looking for devils under every chair and in every corner, though they may well be there. Do not fear them. When you have the Holy Spirit in you, you have all the power you need to resist the influence of evil and loss in your life. The Bible says to resist the devil and he will flee from you. In fact, when you use the name of Jesus, evil has to flee from you. Keep your eyes on the Lord and he will surely lead you in green pastures and beside still waters, just like the 23rd Psalm says.

You can learn to trust God's voice. But if you are not sure of the source of the impressions and ideas you are receiving, by all means ask God. He is trying to speak to and influence you.

As you begin to hear the Lord's voice and tune in to the Spirit of God, you will also begin to recognize when a voice spoken into your mind is not God. But, sometimes you won't. Even though I have been travelling this path for many years, I still sometimes miss it. However, the presence of the Holy Spirit in my life will alert me when I have taken a wrong turn, or heeded a thought that did not come from God.

The way God does this is by making me uneasy, or causing me to feel that something just isn't right. You know the feeling I mean. To your mind, the choice may be clear. You have gone through a decision-making process, usually involving your logic, and arrived at a conclusion regarding something that concerns you. Yet there remains a nagging doubt, or a sense that something is just not right. You don't have complete peace about your plan of action. Chances are you have listened to the wrong spiritual suggestions, which appeal to your mind rather than your spirit where the Holy Spirit resides. Or, it could be that God has something else you should know, and you need to take the time to find out what it is.

Avoid trying to hear God with your logic.

If there is a struggle going on between your head and your heart, get alone with God and have a talk. If you do not stay in tune with God and with your own spirit speaking, your logical mind can override your spirit. Continuing on the path of mere logic, and your own will, usually leads to loss of some kind. It is important to take the time to listen to the Holy Spirit's urging in your heart.

Let me give you an example. When we were living in France, I had arranged with a Canadian home-schooling organization to buy their materials to teach my two daughters while we travelled. I had taken delivery of all the materials needed for the year that we left Canada. In home-schooling you can cover a lot more material in a much shorter time than traditional schools can, so we had finished all the courses sometime in May even including a few months that we took off for travelling and visiting my husband's family in England.

The people at the organization from which we purchased our home-schooling books and materials had urged me to order what we would require for the following year as early as possible to make sure they had stock on the textbooks when we would need them. I went through the catalogues with my children and we chose the programs for their curricula. I filled out the forms and prepared to send them away. Then a funny thing happened. Every time I saw that envelope and told myself that I had to get it in the mail, I would pick it up and look at it, then put it back on the shelf by the door. Something was stopping me from taking the step of mailing it. My head told me sending it away was the right thing to do, but my spirit was saying something else.

So I started talking to myself, reminding myself that it made perfect sense to get on this right away. I let my logic talk me into mailing the order along with a cheque for a hundred dollars for school registration. The books were expected to arrive later in the summer.

The home-schooling organization cashed my cheque. For some reason I could not define, I had a sinking feeling about the whole thing. I could not figure out why I felt so heavy about doing what I had done. No matter how I looked at it, it made sense to me that I should register the children for their school programs at the scheduled time.

The reason for my discomfort soon became clear. A few weeks after my order had gone through we had a meeting with our employers at the estate. They informed us that they had a change in their plans regarding staff and after the end of July they would no longer have work for us. This news came as quite a shock, since we were prepared to remain working for them in France for another year or two. As it turned out, we returned to Canada by that August and our children entered public school in our new hometown. Though I informed the home-schooling people that we would not be using their services and materials the next school year, they were unable to refund my registration fees. Had I listened to the Holy Spirit as he was trying to warn me, I would have saved myself the anxiety I experienced, plus the loss of a hundred dollars.

Practice being in my presence by continually conversing with me. You will soon find that you are hearing me clearly all of the time and my leading is very plain. My sheep know my voice, so listen, my lamb.

God wants to protect us from problems and struggles except when defeating them will help to strengthen our faith. The important thing to remember is that he will guide us through anything and in any situation. We can unequivocally rely on his wisdom and his help.

Stop believing that God wants you to suffer.

I believe that this is a good time to mention that many people are under the mistaken impression that God means for them to suffer and that much of the misery in life is imposed on us by God to teach us something. This could not be further from the truth. God is a good God who wants good things for his children. He does not use sickness, disease, suffering, pain or misery to teach us because he does not need to. The Holy Spirit and the word of God both teach us how we can overcome pain and misery in our lives. We could learn everything we need to know about what God is like and how he works if we were to just read his word.

As a case in point, let me ask you something. What has misery, sickness, or pain taught you so far? Has it led you to become a better person? Has it revealed God's love and care to you? Has it helped you to understand what God is like? I'm guessing the answer is no. Any person with common sense can see that for God to use suffering as a teacher when his word clearly shows us how to avoid or overcome suffering is totally contradictory. The concept that suffering or disease comes from the hands of God for our benefit is also contrary to the character of God. That is why I must stress again that you need to read God's word and find out what he says about himself, so you will recognize the source of good and evil in your life.[1]

But, perhaps you are confused about why you have suffered what you have. As I mentioned earlier, we have an enemy whose mandate is to lead you away from God in any way he can so he can harm you. If you are suffering, the source is clear. It comes from our enemy, not from our loving God. On the other hand, God is our refuge and strength and a very present help in trouble.[2]

Avoid falling into the belief that if things aren't going well for you, God must not be on your side. God is always on your side, always wants the best for you and is always available to help when things don't go right.[3]

Is that you, God, or is it just me?

One of the biggest problems people I know have when it comes to hearing from God, is confusion about whether what they hear is God speaking or just their own thoughts. In order to deal with this, there are a few things to remember. Let's look at these two problems separately.

Be alert for confusion.

First, God is not the author of confusion. [4] It is neither his will nor his plan that we be confused. God's desire is that there be no ambiguity regarding his leading. [5] So if you are confused, either about what you have heard, or about what you should do, remember that God wants you to have clarity. He has very definite plans for your life, so if you are confused about what you should be doing or which direction to go, what to think or believe, or how to behave, then take more time to listen to God's guidance before you act.

Perhaps you need more information. If that is the case, go back to God and ask for more information. Don't stay confused. Study God's word and find out what he has to say about your situation. Demand and expect clarity, then you will be able to act with confidence in whatever God may have for you to do, say, or be.

Was that just *me*?

If you are bewildered about the source of what you hear, whether you heard the voice of God, or just your own thoughts, you will not be likely to take action, will you? Though it rarely happens any more, from time to time I have been confused about God's leading in my life. My head says one thing, my circumstances say something else, my friends tell me what they think, and my heart is hard to hear. Though God will sometimes use circumstances and other people to help lead you, it is important that you first get quiet enough to hear the still, small voice of the Holy Spirit for yourself. Try to go away by yourself for a time, either a few hours, or if need be, a day or more. Focus in on God and ask him to speak to you clearly.

In the name of Jesus, you have the authority to command that the spirit of confusion flee. (It is my understanding that yes, there is a real spirit called confusion. This spirit is obviously not from God, or you would not be having trouble, so you have the authority to command it to cease operating in anything concerning you.)

Doing this is simple and straightforward, not weird in any way. What I usually say is something like, "In the name of Jesus, I command every spirit that is not from Jesus himself, God the Father or the Holy Spirit to flee from me now and to cease trying to influence me in any way." Sometimes I also name the troublesome emotions I am experiencing such as frustration, anger, resentment, confusion, depression, contention, or whatever else I may be feeling. I have no compunction at all about blaming the devil for trouble. He gets away with far too much already. I think you will find, like I do, that immediately the atmosphere is cleared of meddling spiritual activity.

I will expand on the truth of using the name of Jesus in a later chapter, but for now, just know that this works. I will caution you, however, always to treat the name of Jesus with utmost respect and reverence as there is great power in his name.

There is one more step that I took many years ago that revolutionized my life and my ability to hear from God. I spoke to God directly and asked that he speak to me clearly and unmistakably. I also told him that from then on I would continue under the assumption that whenever I felt reasonably sure that it was his voice that I heard, I would act accordingly. I think the Holy Spirit must have breathed a huge sigh of relief, knowing that I chose to trust that I could actually hear God in my own spirit and mind, and would move forward with assurance from there.

When God speaks to us, of course he sounds like us to a certain extent but as a guard against confusion you only need ask yourself if what you hear lines up with God's character and his word. God will not suggest you do anything, believe anything, or act in any way that does not demonstrate love and good will. He will always lead you to create more peace, joy, love and kindness, and less confusion, bitterness, resentment, division or any other negative outcome. This alone is a good guide to live by. Remember that the good stuff comes from God and the bad stuff from the devil.

God wants us to be able to hear and understand him when he speaks. He wants to have a relationship with us. If talking with God always leaves you feeling like you've had a bad telephone connection then you will want to make hearing God clearly a priority in your spiritual life. It can be done, as you will soon discover.

[1] Psalms 145:8-9, 16-19

Psalms 103:1-5, 8

Exodus 34:6-7

Nehemiah 9:17(b)

Jeremiah 9:23-2

John 10:10

[2] Psalms 46:1

[3] Psalm 118:6

Romans 8:31

[4] 1Cor. 14:33

[5] Col. 1:9-10

Journal

At the beginning of this chapter I describe an incident involving driving in a rain storm. As you think about this story, list the parallels between this account and your own life.

In the section called *Don't be superficial* I touch on various ways that our beliefs and behaviours keep God at a distance. Review these ways and describe how your past beliefs or ideas may have interfered with you knowing God better.

God is not impressed when we boast that we've done things our own way without his help. He wants to show us how to do things a better way – his way. As we submit our desires and plans to God he will conform our thinking to his own. If you continuously choose to discuss your plans with God, how will this change your way of doing things?

As intelligent beings, we often have our own ideas about how things should be done and when, yet God always has better ideas than we do. When you choose to follow God's agenda, your life becomes simpler and much less stressful. In what areas of your life can you hand over control to God so you can enjoy the peace that he offers you?

How do you see that doing that will change your life?

God wants to give us the desires of our hearts but he wants to be the one to put those desires in our hearts. He really does want us to be happy, yet our own ideas of how that should work sometimes do not match God's. Why do you think it is important to find out what God's are desires for you?

I once heard the story of a man who never made an important decision in his business without first spending up to three solitary days with God to find out exactly what God's recommendations were. This man was one of the richest people of his day. If you were to not move forward before receiving directions from God, what decisions would this course of action affect?

Working with God is a joint venture, and he delights in helping us achieve our dreams. Our companionship is important to him. Can you think of a time when you followed a dream without asking God to accompany and assist you? How did that go?

God will never force you to turn control of your life over to him even though he knows that it will be better for you. When we insist on controlling our own lives, he will step back and let us. When we do that, we exempt ourselves from accessing his power and support. Explain how you feel about letting God have control of your days and your life.

In this chapter, I bring up the subject of evil spirits in more detail. While the presence of evil is real, there is no need to fear it when you have Jesus by your side. If this is the first time you have been introduced to knowledge of the spirit world and in particular, to evil spirits, how do you feel about learning of their presence?

As you learn to discern God's voice, by contrast the voices from enemy spirits will also be more easily distinguishable. The Holy Spirit will confirm his words to you in different ways. Sometimes it is a sense of conscience, other times a word from a friend. If you look back on your life, can you notice times when the enemy may have tried or succeeded to lead you in a direction that was not from God. What happened?

We have been given logical minds, emotions, and spiritual sensitivity. If we live by using our logical minds and emotions most of the time, we will not learn how to sense God's leading in our spirits. If you find that you are caught in an internal argument, your mind and your spirit may be at odds. When this happens, it is important to spend time listening just to your spirit, while commanding your mind to be quiet. Can you tell of a time in your recent memory that you have experienced this kind of internal clash?

Many of the world's religions teach that God requires that we suffer a lot in order to gain acceptance in his eyes. This teaching is usually based on tradition rather than God's words. What has your experience with this kind of teaching been?

Can you see how the enemy uses deception to cause us to suffer and fail? If we fall prey to falsehoods that demand that we endure misery or tragedy, they force us into our own defeat. Describe how religious or traditional beliefs about suffering, pain, or retribution from God have affected your life.

One of the most common problems that most of us deal with is not knowing if the voice that we hear inside us is God speaking or just our own thoughts? Have you ever had that experience? The fact is that God speaks to us through our own thoughts. Tell about a time when you know that you heard God speak to you in your own thoughts.

One of the tactics that the enemy uses to prevent us from knowing God and having a relationship with him is to confuse us. Since confusion cannot be from God, we can be assured that we can go to God to seek relief from confusion. If you are dealing with uncertainty now, I urge you to command that the spirit of confusion cease harassing you. Use the name of Jesus and you access the power of God, then that spirit must leave. Go ahead and try it and record what happens.

I found that probably the most profound breakthrough that I had when learning to hear God speak in my life was when I made the decision to believe I heard God when I wondered if it had. Whenever I felt reasonable sure it was God I heard and not my own head or some other voice, I would act on that. God honoured my sincerity and determination and he will do the same for you. Reflect on making this choice for yourself.

SIX

Going Forward

Some years ago, a friend told me the tragic story of her sister Susan's life. Without apparent warning, Susan's husband left her and their four small children for another woman. Susan and her family lived on a farm in a rural area, and her wayward husband moved in with this woman, who lived on a farm just across their country road. Susan and the children watched in horror as their husband and father carried on his illicit affair before their eyes.

Susan did everything she could to restore her marriage and family for the sake of her children, but her husband made it clear that he had no interest in continuing a relationship with any of them. The family was torn apart and the children's hearts were broken. At length Susan came to realize that any hope of a happy ending with his man would never come to pass, and to save the children from further suffering, she decided to move away from the area to a small nearby city. Eventually, her husband divorced her. After all the legal wrangling wrapped up, Susan came out of the situation with little money to help set up a new home for her family.

My friend told me of these happenings when I saw her from time to time. My heart broke for Susan and her troubles and I prayed for help to come to her through this difficult situation. Since she didn't live near me and I didn't know her well, after a while I thought of her only in passing and wondered how she was doing. Then that summer, a few months after the break-up and Susan's subsequent move, she came to my mind again. I sensed that God was speaking to me to send Susan some money. Since I didn't have much cash to spare myself, I quickly dismissed the idea as impossible. This went on for a week or more, with the thought coming to my mind now and then.

Not long after, my husband had his annual vacation break from his job and we planned to take our family on a camping trip. As I loaded the little camper van with our gear, sleeping bags, groceries, swim toys and summer clothes, I again had the thought that I should send Susan some money. By this time, I was pretty sure that this was no random thought. The Holy Spirit was trying to tell me something. When I asked what I should do, he spoke into my mind that I should send Susan one hundred dollars. Because I didn't feel I could do that, I put off responding.

We left on our vacation, travelling around and camping, and the longer I was away, the more insistent the voice in my spirit became. Rather like having a blister on your heel where the more you walk, the more it bothers you, the more I resisted sending Susan the money, the more God nudged me. I have to admit that I was beginning to feel a bit nagged over it. As the days of our vacation slid by, I began to look forward to going home, just so I could send Susan that one hundred dollars and stop thinking about it.

Coming home from camping with our children in a van full of dirt, pine needles and grubby clothes, I felt worn out and in dire need of a shower. But the first thing I did when I came through the door of my house was to rush to my desk, find Susan's address, write the cheque and mail it to her. Finally, I felt at peace. I actually sensed God smiling at me for having obeyed his instructions. I didn't know how I would replace the money in my own budget, but I don't remember it ever being an issue.

Nothing happened for several weeks and I had almost forgotten about it when one day I received a little card in the mail from Susan. She thanked me for my gift of the money. She also told me that it was the exact amount she had needed to finish making a down payment on a new home for herself and her children. Suddenly, I saw the whole picture.

Susan went to God and asked him to provide the down payment for her new home. God came to me to be one of those who would help him answer her request. Why did he choose me? Simple. I knew of her situation through my friend. I knew how to hear God when he asked me to send her some money. And he knew that I would have enough, since he would see to it that I did.

Sometimes I think talking to God would be a lot easier if he just showed up and sat down on the edge of the bed beside me while I'm pulling on my socks in the morning. He might say something like, "Hey, what are you doing today?" And I could answer him. We could talk over whatever problems I needed his help with and he could give me his insight on how he sees my situation. I could mention how impressed and thankful I am with how he has recently worked things out for me. It seems that would make the whole relationship so much easier - for me, at least. However, there are ways to have this kind of relationship with God that are even easier and more immediate.

God uses more than one way to communicate with us. The reason is simple. If one way is not working and he's not getting through to us, he will use another way. Remember that God wants to communicate with us much more than we know.

Some of these ways are through the following:

- an audible voice
- conversation with God or prayer
- dreams
- the Bible
- other things we read or watch
- other people
- circumstances and situations
- prophetic words spoken out loud by yourself or others
- visions
- inner peace or unrest
- your own past experience
- your natural talents and abilities
- spiritual gifts
- the inner voice or inner knowing

The audible voice

Let's look at these. First, there is the audible voice. This would be an actual voice you hear with your external ears. God seldom uses this method of interaction because, frankly, it would scare the daylights out of most of us. Though I think I have only ever heard God speak to me audibly in a word or two, there have been other times when what I heard was so clear that I wondered if anyone else in the room heard it. Since no one showed any signs of having heard anything, I had to conclude that I was the only one.

There are many ways that I speak to my children. First, there is the audible voice. For the sensitive heart I almost never need to use this because the Holy Spirit inside gives the message. Sometimes when my children are in great anguish or great danger I speak audibly since this may be the only way to get through the pain and external noise and get someone's attention.

If your attention is already tuned in to the voice of God, you might never hear him talk to you audibly. But there may come a time that God uses an audible voice because that is what you need to hear.

Prayer

Second – prayer. Though not a new concept, for many it remains a mystery. What is prayer? How do you pray? What do you say? What can you expect when you pray? These and other questions often plague us when it comes to prayer. Not finding answers to these and other questions has often prevented people from pursuing and finding a deep relationship with God that they desire.

Put simply, prayer is nothing more than talking with God. For this reason, I have not used the word "prayer" itself throughout this program, since many people have difficulty getting past seeing prayer as too religious, therefore out of reach for them. Talking to God is as easy as talking to yourself. If you assume God is with you as he says he is, and in you when you are a believer in Jesus, then you can go ahead and talk to him like he is in the room with you, because he is. Wherever you go, he is there, too.

Prayer, or talking to God, does not need to take place in a formal setting, using formal words or prescribed lines. You don't have to wear special garments, cover your head, show up in church or talk in whispers. You don't have to assume any special posture, perform special rituals or have any particular title to approach God. Prayer is as simple and as natural as breathing, only with the consciousness that God is with you.

Whatever you want to talk about is okay with God. Anything that is important to you is important to God. If you just want to check in and say hi, God is fine with that. In fact, if you are uneasy talking with God, that is a good place to start. Remember that God wants a relationship with you. He is gentle and kind and will not push you around or force you to smarten up before he will talk with you. He always accepts you just as you are. You don't have to clean up your life before you talk to God. Once you have begun a two-way relationship with God, he will help you to change in ways you may never have dreamed of and will make your life better and better.

God is happy to have you show up no matter what your state of mind or attitude. He is even happy to have you talk to him when you are angry with him. He can handle anything you dish out. He is strong and steadfast and sincere. In the next chapter we will go into more depth on the subject of talking to and hearing God but for now, let's move on.

Dreams

Another way that God speaks to us is through our dreams. If you are one of those people who frequently remember dreams, you may find that God uses them to communicate with you. Often when I have been troubled about something or seeking God's direction for a situation, particularly if I have not been able to take the time to get quiet with God, I will ask him to show me what I need to know in a dream.

Though it may require some help to interpret your dreams, they are a way for God to sidestep your conscious mind and speak directly to your spirit. I have found that sometimes my dreams will stay in my conscious mind all day or even for several days. When this happens I assume that God is trying to tell me something and try to take the time to think through the dream, asking God to interpret it for me so I can benefit from its message to me. Another method you can use is to write down your dreams and ask God to show you how to interpret them. Or, each time you remember a dream, ask God if he has a message for you in the dream. It could be for direction, warning, clarification or knowledge of things to come.

If you don't typically remember your dreams, but occasionally find that one survives into the light of day, you might take a little time to examine it for what God may be trying to tell you and ask him to bring to mind what he wants you to notice. Ask him to help you remember it and get his message across to your conscious mind. However, if you never remember dreaming, don't worry about it. God will communicate with you in ways that you can understand.

The Bible

Perhaps the easiest and most common way that God speaks to his children is through his written word, the Bible. As believers have discovered throughout history, reading the word of God connects you with God in a way that nothing else does. If you are new to reading God's word or if you have had trouble understanding it, then you only need to ask for the help of the Holy Spirit to open your mind to comprehend what God is saying to you through his words. I would also recommend that you go to a bookstore that specializes in Bibles and ask for help in choosing a version that is written in modern language and is easy for you to follow. The Bible has been updated over the centuries to reflect the language uses of the day, but the message and intent have remained virtually unchanged. Modern scholars have spent thousands of hours translating the texts from the original Greek and Hebrew manuscripts to capture the exact nuances of the original meanings.

The great thing about the Bible is that you can pick it up and start reading anywhere and you will find that it feeds your soul. The Bible is full of directions for living a successful and fulfilling life. It alone contains the secrets of the ages for life, love, and sweetness in every area of existence. If you are a beginner, it may surprise you that I recommend that you not start at the beginning, but rather at the New Testament. This is the story of what life was like after Jesus was born. Reading the accounts of Jesus himself and what he encountered as he walked the earth will give you a clearer picture of what God the Father is like. Jesus himself said, 'if you have seen me, you have seen the Father, because I and the Father are one.'

The Bible holds an inexhaustible supply of wisdom and spiritual knowledge. Once again I urge you to put aside any prejudices or preconceived ideas you may have regarding reading the Bible and approach it with fresh eyes. Once you have decided to read it with an open mind, you automatically allow the Holy Spirit to reveal the meaning of its words to you. As you spend more time reading, I am convinced that you will also begin to notice there is more to the Bible than just a bunch of words on paper. There is actual spiritual power in the word of God that you can use to change your life and situations around you. But first, you must be open to the wisdom contained in the pages of this book, and you must be willing to learn, allowing the Holy Spirit to enlighten your understanding of the spiritual truths found therein.

I recommend that you spend some time each day, or at least several times a week just reading God's word. As you read, God will speak into your spirit what you need to hear for the day or for your situation. Often if you go to God with a problem or request, he will answer you through his word.

Just recently, when I went to bed, I picked up my Bible. As I was quite tired I simply asked God what he wanted me to read. Instantly a scripture reference came to my mind so I looked it up. I realized that the passage resonated with my situation so I read it twice before closing the book. Then I picked up my pastor's notes from the previous Sunday. The notes referred to the very same passage I had just seen in the Bible. That was even more interesting. After putting down those notes, I picked up another book and opened it to where my bookmark had been placed. On that very page, there was reference to the same passage I had found in the Bible. Within a half hour, God had told me the same thing three times. Obviously, he really wanted me to know it. This is a good example of how God will speak to you through his word.

Books, articles, movies

This brings me to the next method that God uses to speak to us – through other materials we read or watch. I'm sure you have had the experience where you are reading something in a book or magazine or even on the internet, and suddenly a thought seems to jump off the page at you. It stands out like a beacon. Maybe after you finish the piece and walk away, that thought keeps coming to mind, or you go back and re-read it a few times and each time it makes a deeper impression. This is an example of how God speaks to you through other media.

As I have mentioned before, God will use whatever means he can to touch your life. When you have troubles or problems to deal with, or need answers, God is there to help. He has an imagination and a sense of humour. We know this because we are made in his image and we have those traits. You can hardly blame God for wanting to change things from time to time just to keep your attention.

Other People

I look forward to seeing how God will interact with me next. On occasion he speaks to me through other people. Sometimes you have to be on the alert to tell when God is speaking to you through others. Other times it can be very obvious. I have often had another believer come to me and tell me that I have been on his or her mind. This person may ask what I am going through and express encouragement or support for me. Or they may ask if they can pray for me, and when they do, the words they speak apply directly to my situation because God is speaking through them.

Speakers

Another common way that God communicates with you is through the words of a speaker. It is not uncommon at all to hear someone speak and feel like he or she must have been reading your journal or your mail. What they say can be so "right on" for your situation that it is uncanny. But you have to remember that God knows you intimately. He knows your troubles and he knows your needs, so what is stopping him from impressing that speaker to talk about that answer for your problems?

It is important that you don't dismiss happenings like this. You must be attentive to what the Holy Spirit is trying to impart so that you can live a successful and masterful life. One word of caution here, though – be sure that you trust the source of any message you may feel comes from God. There are lots of people who say they speak from God or have a message for you from God, but unless you know those people well or trust their track record, by all means take those impartations with a grain of salt until you have been able either to verify the source or you have had the same message from one or two other sources whom you trust. Many people have gone off the rails by listening to a charismatic or persuasive character without first doing due diligence on their credentials. In other words, just because someone says he speaks for God, doesn't necessarily mean it's the truth. Check things out before making any moves.

Circumstances

Another way that God leads us is through circumstances and situations. To be frank, these are often harder to recognize and not the best method of connecting with God. There are two things to remember here. The first is that sometimes things happen in a certain sequence or in ways we don't expect because our plans are flawed or are just made with insufficient information. There are times when God will orchestrate events or a situation in our lives because he sees the bigger picture and his goals are different than ours.

How many times have you realized that things you planned didn't work out as you planned them, but if they hadn't happened the way they did, you would not have had a certain experience, or met a person you needed to meet? When we submit our lives into God's hands for him to lead as he sees fit, we can go ahead with our plans, but we must let God make whatever changes he desires to make. Once you let God be God in your life and just respond to his leading, he will lead you more and more into the life he wants for you. The important thing to remember here is to allow God to make changes in your plans without resisting or insisting on having things your way. God will not force you to comply with his will for you, but I can assure you that life will go much better if you do. He won't actively cause you to suffer, but you, by your own stubborn choices, can place yourself out of his divine protection and become subject to needless attacks from the enemy. When you go along with God, he goes along with you. There are lots of perks involved when you do things God's way.

The other point I want to make regarding circumstances and situations is: try not to second-guess God. This often happens with people who do not know God well or who don't actually take the time to listen to God for themselves. If you are always unclear about God's involvement in your life, you may be tempted to try to figure out how he will work in your circumstances. Doing this is like walking around with your eyes closed when the lights are on. All you really have to do is open your eyes and you will see where you are going, but if you don't, you will end up feeling your way around, trying to guess what's going on around you. This is an inferior way of understanding and hearing God.

God has given us so many methods to understand him clearly and concisely that it makes no sense not to use them. If you don't spend the time getting to know God and learning to hear his voice, then you have no choice but to stumble around blindly, merely guessing at what's going on. It doesn't have to be this way.

Please don't let pride or arrogance keep God from working for you. To do so means choosing to miss out on an array of opportunities and blessing that God is waiting to share with you. Not only that, but because we can never know enough about all the forces at work in the universe, we need God to help us. It is good to know that when you need him you can call and he will answer you.

As you learn to hear his voice and heed his leading, it will become easier and easier as time goes on. If you are nervous about jumping out and believing God for big things in your life, then begin to learn to trust God for little things. For example, when I go shopping or to the city for the day where I know there will be lots of traffic and full parking lots, I always ask God to find me a parking spot close to where I need to stop. I've never paid much attention as to how he gets me great parking spots, but either he gives me the idea to go a certain way, or turn at a certain corner, or he just influences someone to leave about the time I come along. In either case, as I trust him and he always finds good parking spots for me.

You could ask him to help you find just the right pair of shoes for your new outfit, or lead you to the right colour of paint for your living room. Maybe you are having trouble with a child or a co-worker. Ask God to help you by showing you what you can do to improve the situation. You can ask him to change your circumstances if that is the right solution.

Prophecy

The dictionary defines the word "prophecy" as "the foretelling or prediction of what is to come or a divinely inspired utterance or revelation." I believe that prophecy is simply hearing what God says and speaking it out. Sometimes God speaks to us prophetically and tells us what is to come or reveals something to us that we could not see with our limited viewpoint or experience. Sometimes what he has to tell us is purely for our own personal benefit, and other times it is to be shared with others to uplift and encourage them. For example, God spoke the following to me one day and I recorded it in my journal.

I long to shepherd my people. A shepherd cares for the sheep, provides the best for them, protects them, guards their health, and leads them to the best possible situations and conditions. I will do the same for you when you continue in me. When you join my "flock," you can expect all those things. I will even go after you when you wander off or drift away. I am not willing for any harm to come to you or that anything makes you sick, or anyone perish. No, I want the very best for you always. I came to bring you abundant life and it is here for the taking to those who choose to follow me. As you renew your mind with my word and truth you will find it more and more simple to access everything you need and want from my storehouse of abundance.

Let me give you another example of how God speaks prophetically. When we first moved to Europe, you could say we went on a wing and a prayer. That would be airplane wings and lots of prayers. We had sold our house, stored our belongings, and taken off for an uncertain future. My sister and her husband had been gracious enough to let us use their place in Switzerland as our home base while trying to figure out what to do next.

In the time leading up to our departure from Canada, I had felt a leading to go to the Burgundy region of eastern France, but had no particular plan for a specific town to go to nor what to do once there. We arranged to rent a holiday home in a tiny village where we stayed for three weeks in January. During this time we explored the surrounding region and my husband looked for work. Day after day we set out. Our holiday flat was made of stone and as the winter is cold and damp in France, the place never felt warm. We spent a small fortune on heating bills and still wore our winter coats indoors most of the time. We found that it was much less expensive to put gas in our borrowed car and warm up with its efficient heater as we drove around than try to heat our stone cavern of a house.

After many days of travelling the countryside, looking for work and being turned down, we became quite discouraged. One evening while cooking supper, my husband and I talked over our options, trying to decide what to do next. Suddenly, I said, "It's not going to work out like we think it will, but it will work out!" Instantly, I knew, that though those words came from my mouth, it was not me who spoke them, but the Holy Spirit. Because I was being sensitive to him, he was able to speak through me to give us the encouragement we needed. He was right, of course. It didn't work out like we thought it would, but it did work out. We never found work or a home in the Burgundy, but rather found an excellent situation in Provence.

Visions

Another way that God speaks to people today (and has throughout history) is through visions. A vision can be something you see with your eyes or something that is only seen in your mind or with your imagination. There are essentially three different kinds of vision experiences. First, there is what may be referred to as a trance. Your five senses will be temporarily suspended so that you are not aware whether what you are seeing is in the natural or not because it appears so real. This kind of vision does not really require much faith since it is obvious what God is trying to tell you. I believe that God uses this kind of vision when he needs you to follow very specific instructions.

The second type of vision is sometimes called an "open vision." When this happens you would be completely aware of the natural world around you, yet seeing a vision at the same time. There may be times when the Lord will open your spiritual eyes to allow you to see into the spirit realm. People have been known to see Jesus, angels or even demonic spirits in this kind of vision, while still being aware of their surroundings.

The third type of vision is a spiritual vision. This type is close to what you might see in your imagination and in fact, God often uses our imaginations to help us see things he wants us to know. You can usually differentiate this from your imagination if what you see is not something you would normally think up on your own. In times of deep prayer or meditation, God might bring pictures to your mind that help to illustrate what he is trying to tell you. At times like this, you can be aware of your surroundings but so focused on what is going on in your imagination that you don't notice anything else. If someone were to nudge you, you would feel it and respond. Think of this type of vision as seeing with your spiritual eyes. You are not in a trance.

A spiritual vision requires the most faith because you may question whether what you see is from God or just your own imagination. The best way to deal with these questions is to ask God for clarification. I decided long ago that if I thought what I saw was from God, I would act as though it definitely came from him. Whatever the vision might be telling me, I would believe. But it is important to remember that first I have demanded that no influence or spirit other than God be able to touch or affect me while I am meditating or conversing with God. This provides me with a level of protection while opening my spirit to what the Holy Spirit wants to show me.

As you open your heart to God, he will communicate with you in the way he chooses. If you are a visual person, used to exercising your imagination, he will likely use a visual style of speaking with you. If you have never seen any sort of vision in your life, then you are in the majority. I just want you to be aware that seeing visions in any of the ways I have described is possible, so if you have a vision, do not be alarmed, be thankful. God wants to tell you something. If you are unclear what the vision means just ask him. He wants you to understand clearly and not have to guess what he's trying to say.

Inner Peace or Unease

Another way that God uses to communicate with us is through our senses or feelings. This type of communication is a little more difficult to explain so I will give an example.

Some years ago, I had a job at a restaurant downtown in the city where I lived. I liked the work and people with whom I worked, but was only able to work part-time and found that I needed more hours to make a higher income. There was a restaurant in a neighbourhood nearby where I lived that advertised for help, so I applied there and got a job working more hours. After several weeks of working both jobs, the owner of the neighbourhood restaurant found out I was also working downtown, so he approached me and suggested that I quit the downtown job and work full-time in his restaurant. I had the sense that this was not really the right thing for me to do and I didn't want to leave my downtown job, but since the neighbourhood job was closer to home it made more sense to work there rather than farther away. So I quit working downtown.

During the first shift I worked at the neighbourhood restaurant, I had the most terrible sense that I had done the wrong thing. All evening I worked with a sinking feeling inside. Even though I told myself that logically I had made the right decision, my heart knew that I had made the wrong one. It wasn't long until the situation played itself out. The owner of the restaurant did not treat his staff well, and one by one they quit and found work elsewhere. One night I went in to work to find myself the only staff member to serve a whole restaurant and lounge. The owner screamed at me to hurry up and serve all the evening's customers, and when I couldn't keep up, he screamed at me some more. At the end of the evening I quit. The working conditions were unbearable. A few days later I drove past the restaurant and saw a big "Closed" sign on the door. Now I was out of a job entirely. The downtown restaurant had replaced me by now and I had to go looking for a new job.

My problem was not that I got into a bad situation, but that God had been trying to warn me not to go there and I ignored the sense of unrest in my spirit. Often when faced with decisions, we do what our head says, while our heart is saying something else. My advice is: ignore your heart at your own peril. This is where the Holy Spirit will speak to you but often he does so without words. He will use your emotions to lead you on the right path.

When you have a choice to make, a good way to utilize this concept is to imagine yourself on each path separately and see how you feel about each one. For example, if you are trying to decide between two different jobs or two different houses, whether to go somewhere or not, try imagining yourself in each separate situation. Begin by asking for God's direction; then ask yourself how you feel when you are trying on that situation. Do you feel uncomfortable or peaceful? Does something just not feel right or do you feel a lift of joy? It won't be long until you know exactly the right thing to do. Having a sense of peace about a decision is one of the most reliable methods of knowing God's will for your life. When you seek that sense of peace about your decisions, you can be sure you are on the right path.

Past Experiences

God will also use your past experiences to speak to you. We humans are usually not very good at heeding in this area, which is why history repeats itself. How often have you repeated the behaviour that someone else has failed at but do it anyway since you have convinced yourself that you have superior knowledge and ability and will get different results? Have you repeated your own behaviours, only to end up with the same unwanted consequences? Remember those times you banged your head with your fist and moaned, "Why did I do that again? I already knew it wouldn't work." The Bible says that as a dog returns to his vomit, so a fool repeats his folly[1]. Yuck! Don't go there.

If you find yourself reminded of past experiences, it might be that God is trying to speak to you or warn you not to go down that road again. You would be wise to listen and heed the warning.

Experiences of Others

God can also teach us or speak to us through the experiences of other people. You may hear someone speak about some incident they have had and suddenly you identify. You might say, "That happened to me, too," then find out what they did and learn from it. Or you may be in a situation where you don't know what to do, and hearing someone tell of his or her experience suddenly helps you see possibilities for yourself. But remember not to take off after something just because someone else did. First take the time to seek God and get confirmation from him before making a move.

You might find that sometimes this process also works in reverse. You think you know what God is saying to you, but you are not sure. Then a person will come into your life, or someone will say something that confirms what you feel is God's direction for you. God loves it when we act in faith, so even if you make a mistake, God is still there to help you move on or to learn from your actions and find a new direction.

Your talents and abilities

Using our natural talents and abilities is one of the more obvious ways that God speaks; yet so often we miss this vital piece of the puzzle. God has given each of us a unique set of talents and natural abilities with the intent that we use them to make our distinct contribution to our world. As we grow up, we are taught to conform to the social setting into which we were born. This is a good thing if it teaches us how to function in cooperation with others and fit into our own culture. The problem with the mass enculturation that occurs in school and other institutions is that it tends to force us to sublimate our natural tendencies in order to fit in. Rather than being taught to develop our strengths and natural abilities, we are too often taught to work on our weaknesses and not get carried away with our favourite things.

On one hand, this type of learning ignores the fact that we are not all the same and trying to force us to be is useless. Why do you think that so many adults spend years finding their own passion in life, or developing their true loves? As children, our natural characteristics have often been sanded down so that we are more and more like each other.

On the other hand, by not developing our natural talents to their best, we deprive others of the gifts that we have to bring to the world. There is a reason we all have different gifts and abilities. God created us this way so that we can share what we have with those who have not. By that I mean, none of us is fabulously accomplished in every area of life. We all have strengths and we all have areas of difficulty. But your strength may exactly match my weakness, and my weakness may perfectly complement your strength. This is why we need each other. We all have something different to bring to the table at this time in history to the people with whom we come in contact.

Knowing this, God will lead you in the realm for which he has given you certain talents and abilities. God will always lead you more and more into being your true self. He created you to be you, so when you are living your life to your truest potential according to your giftings, then you are most pleasing to God. If you wonder what to do with your life, ask yourself what your natural talents are and use those.

The way I look at it is that God puts desires in your heart to do the things he has planned for you to do. When you pursue those passions and desires, then you are following the leadings God has placed within you. His purpose is for you to be your most happy, and make the best contribution to your world. It is a fantastic system when we work with it. When I am following after the desires of my heart and producing things like my art and this program, then I am making my contribution to the world. When you purchase something that I am contributing it is because it fills a need in your life, or because it provides you with something you cannot create yourself.

Our gifts suggest a lot about our calling in life. By tracing what an individual has usually been preoccupied with, many times gifts are easy to identify. Some enjoy talking with people, others enjoy working with tools and tangible objects, still others prefer working with abstracts like numbers, words or images. Some like helping people; others use their bodies in sports or theatre or their voices in music.

Our natural gifts are also traceable from our personality attributes. Each of us has inborn personality traits, a unique combination of strengths and weaknesses. Strengths promote the realization of our natural abilities while weaknesses hinder them. Correctly identifying one's personality traits is crucial in understanding and maximizing one's natural abilities. An important point to note is that there is no personality combination that is better or worse than another.

Because the subject of spiritual gifts and the inner knowing are such big topics, I will cover them in depth in the next chapter.

[1]Proverbs 26:11

Journal

When I learned about the plight of my friend's friend Susan, I sensed that God was urging me to send Susan some money to help her. Have you ever had an experience in which you have sensed God compelling you to a certain course of action? Tell what that was like.

God uses many different methods to speak to us. Can you think why he chooses to use different approaches with different people? Have you had God speak to you in any of the ways listed in this chapter? What was that like?

God seldom uses an audible voice to speak to most people, yet many have heard him speak this way. How would you feel if you heard God speak to you in a voice that is capable of being heard by your external ears?

Prayer is, in essence, talking to God and listening for his replies. It is a two-way conversation. What has your prior experience with prayer been like? Have you found it fulfilling or frustrating or exciting?

In your view, what would your ideal prayer life be like?

From the beginning of time, God has used dreams to communicate with people yet in our modern-day culture, little attention is paid to dreams that occur when we sleep. Here is an exercise to help you realize more meaning from your dreams. Next time you wake with the memory of a dream, jot down a few notes to help you retain the images that occurred in the dream. Now, ask God if there is something he wants you to know through the dream. You might also ask him if what you dreamed is a message from him, information from your own mind, or a warning about the enemy is trying to do. He will bring to mind what he wants you to know. Make note of what you find out.

The Bible is a reliable source of information about God, the spirit world, and everyday life. I recommend that you begin to read it regularly, preferably everyday. God uses his words in the Bible to speak to us about situations that we encounter daily. In whatever part of the book you may be reading, God may make certain passages 'leap out' at you or seem particularly significant. What you see may be the answer to what you seek. Try taking some time now to read the Bible and write down anything significant that you come across.

When we seek God's help for our lives, he uses whatever he can to bridge the gap between him and us and to answer our questions and pleas. It is not unusual for God to uses books, articles or movies to speak into our lives. If this has happened to you, can you recall what you read or heard that made a noticeable or immediate difference for you?

God often uses other people in our lives to speak what he wants us to know. Though it is important to remember that not everything others say to us comes from the mind of God, if you do sense that he is using someone in your life to speak to you, you should consider what those people are saying. Better still is to take what others have said and take it to God and someone in a mentorship or leadership position in your life and get a 'second opinion'. Can you think of a time when you recognize that God spoke to you through others, and tell what happened?

Circumstances and situations are sometimes orchestrated by God to position us to hear him, or so that he may get our attention. Though it may be difficult to recognize such times, can you think of any circumstances that occurred in your life when you now see that God had been trying to speak to you?

Prophecy is usually considered akin to telling the future, and sometimes that is exactly what it is. Other times, though, it is simply hearing what God is saying and using your own voice to speak it. Sometimes God surprises us by speaking through our own mouths what we need to hear. This often happens when we are in conversation with others. Suddenly, we hear ourselves say something that we know did not originate with our own thoughts. If you can remember any instances of this happening in your life, tell about it here.

In Psalms 23, God is compared to a shepherd and us to his sheep. Jesus also compared himself to a shepherd and used sheep to illustrate what we are like. Using this analogy, can you see how a shepherd cares for the needs of his sheep by looking after details of life like rest, food and protection? How does this translate into your life?

Jesus said in John 10:27, "My sheep hear my voice, and I know them, and they follow me." This statement is a clear indication that we can expect to hear God's voice when we become one of Jesus' 'flock'. If you have not made the ultimate choice to believe in Jesus as your direct connection with God, now is the time. You can confirm your decision by filling in this declaration:

I, _____ do now make the life-changing decision to become a believer in and a follower of Jesus Christ. I understand that Jesus has paid the penalty required for me to become one of God's own children. I choose this day, _____ to be a child of God through Jesus Christ so that he will know me and I will hear his voice speaking to me.

Signed, _____.

How do you feel about making this important decision?

In this chapter, there are several types of visions mentioned that God may use to show us what he wants us to know. As you read about the different types of visions, do you recall having any of these? Can you express what happened both in the vision and as a result of it?

One of the most common ways that God uses to communicate with us is through sense of peace or unease. Using this method to clarify God's leading in your life will make it easier for you to hear him. Try now to employ this means of distinguishing his plans in some area of your own life where you require wisdom or leading and write about that situation here.

God sometimes uses our past experiences or the situations or experiences of others to show us what we need to know about our current circumstances. Can you think of a time when something in your past, or something that happened to someone else, had a powerful or meaningful effect on you?

Our personalities, gifts, talents and abilities are an effective means to lead us on the right paths for our lives. If you have sensed or experienced God's leading in your life through your natural abilities and talents, give an example of that here.

SEVEN

Going Deeper

When I was a teenager growing up on a prairie farm, I owned a little brown and white pinto horse named Bobby. He was old and smart and sometimes pretty ornery, and when I turned his head toward home after chasing steers from one pasture to another at the instruction of my dad, he had the fastest walk of any horse anyone had ever seen. Though smaller than our family's other horses, his stride always set us way ahead of my siblings, so much that I often had to rein him in to wait for the other riders to catch up.

My sister and brothers and I were members of a local 4-H Horse Club, the brainchild of my mother, who was also the club's leader. When I was fifteen I received a brand new saddle for Christmas. To be honest, I was a bit surprised to receive this valuable gift, since, though I was a good rider I was not a particularly passionate one. To me, being involved with horses and cattle was just something our family did, not something I loved to do. I used my saddle for the next couple of years and enjoyed the new leather, the cushioned seat and the fact that I actually owned something of such value.

Then I left home to go to university and after a few years Bobby was sold to some other family. My saddle took up a place in the shop out of the weather, waiting for the day I would use it again. I still own that saddle. It still sits in the shop on my parents' farm. I have never sold it for a variety of reasons, and still enjoy that fact that it is there in case I might one day need it.

When we decide to link up with Jesus and invite the Holy Spirit to become our own personal coach, mentor, and comforter, we become part of God's own family. It is like an adoption and, as one of the family we are in line to receive gifts from our Father. These gifts are spiritual in nature and are far superior to material gifts. In fact, they often transcend the world's natural laws. As with other gifts, you don't need any special qualifications to receive them, only a willingness to be one of God's kids. Your age, education, career background, past history, personality or gender makes no difference at all to your eligibility.

The purpose for receiving these special gifts is to fulfill God's purpose in your life, and to have something to offer to benefit the lives of others. Each of us as a believer has special assignments from God to be accomplished during our lifetime, and our spiritual gifts will help us accomplish them. Though some gifts put the bearer into a more public position than others, no gift is better than another.

Those who are familiar with these particular gifts from God find them comfortable and delightful. However, if you are not so familiar with them you may be find yourself moving into unknown territory. Let me assure you that you have nothing to fear. What you will soon learn is that there is nothing weird or freaky about how God interacts with us; there are just people who pass judgments without knowledge or experience of the supernatural. Since you have come this far in this program, I am sure that you are a sincere seeker of all the God has made available to you for leading a successful life. By now, you know enough to set aside any preconceived ideas about things you may have heard from others who don't have enough experience to be reliable sources of information. Please have patience and let me lead you into this new territory.

The supernatural has been part of my life for nearly as long as I can remember. I began to seek after God as a young child and my life-long journey has led me into some fascinating and exciting experiences and places. Let me assure you that what you are about to learn comes directly from the Bible. I didn't make this up. I also want to reassure you that there are millions of believers all over the world today for whom accessing and drawing experiences from the supernatural resources I am about to describe is as natural as breathing. You are not alone if this is new to you, and you will not be alone when it is as familiar and comfortable as your favourite pair of slippers.

The spiritual gifts that you receive may include one or more of the following:

- special wisdom, obviously greater than you would have on your own
- specific knowledge regarding certain situations or problems in the lives of those with whom you come into contact that you would have no way of knowing in the natural
- faith beyond what you could muster on your own
- the ability to pray for or lay hands on the sick and frequently see them healed
- working miracles that are not humanly possible
- being able to prophesy what is to come or have special insight into what God is saying for encouragement and support of others

- a supernatural ability to see or discern beings in the spirit world, including evil or demonic spirits and angelic spirits
- speaking in tongues or languages that you have never learned in the natural and do not understand the meaning or translation of with your natural mind
- being able to interpret or translate without prior knowledge the messages in diverse tongues delivered by others or yourself

In addition to those spiritual gifts, God also gives us each special abilities and talents that conform to our natural personalities, to make it clear to us how he would like us to spend our lives. The reason that we have been given these gifts or abilities is so that we will share them with the rest of God's family and those who are still seeking spiritual truth. These include:

- the assignment and skill to teach others
- the ability to encourage and uplift others
- the freedom to give generously
- the desire and capacity for practical service to others
- leadership qualities
- a heart of mercy and caring and doing it cheerfully
- special knowledge and skill to help others begin and build organizations, particularly churches or groups of believers
- the ability to speak in public, to inspire and expound
- preaching the gospel and travelling to other people groups to share what God has shown you
- leading in small-group situations, such as acting as a pastor

in the way a shepherd leads and guides

- administration and business ability
- helping others in practical, useful ways, often serving in the background to help things run smoothly.

Spiritual gifts equip each of us to do tasks that may be beyond our natural ability and can work independently of our natural gifts. Or they can enhance your natural skills to accomplish more than you could through your own efforts.

In the beginning it may not be clear to you what special gifts God has given you. A good first step would be to ask him. If you recognize yourself in any of the gifts mentioned above, that could be a clue. If you don't figure this out right away, or if you make a mistake, don't worry about it now. It will gradually become clear to you as you seek God's will for your life. You may save yourself time later if you get alone with God now and see what he tells you, but if the answer is slow in coming to you, rest assured that it will become clearer over time. The more you seek God for his calling on your life, the more obvious your own spiritual gifts will become.

You can receive a spiritual gift when you become a believer, and sometimes that gift turns your life in a completely new direction. Your natural abilities, which may have guided your life before, now decrease in value as you follow the leading of God through your spiritual gifts. For example, I know a young man who worked in retail and had the intention of becoming a manager of a large retail chain store or moving into upper management within the organization. When he decided to let God tell him what direction he should take with his life, rather than following his own inclinations, he discovered that God had given him a gift for being a pastor. With this new knowledge, he left his job, entered a training school to learn how to maximize his gift and now is working toward becoming a chaplain in the armed forces. God had a different plan for him, and he may have a different plan for you than what you have previously envisioned. The important thing to remember is that you must be willing to accept God's direction. God always has a better idea and a better plan for you. No matter what you are doing now, or what direction your life is taking, when you get in line with God's plan you will find much more happiness and fulfillment than you, until now, had ever dreamed possible.

When you know what your gifts are, or what God is calling you to do, it may necessitate a complete change of direction for your life, too. You may realize quite suddenly that God's true purpose for your life is to do something entirely different than you have done before. I encourage you to take the time to be sure before making any drastic decisions, but if you search you own heart and seek the heart of God, you should experience a certainty what you are to do. This is one of the ways that God communicates with us.

Don't be concerned if you don't understand where this new road may take you. Usually God only reveals the first steps, allowing you to learn to trust him for what is to come. There are a couple of reasons why God does things this way. The first is that we are often tempted to take the reins into our own hands and try to do what God has called us to under our own strength and with our own plans. The second reason is that by only revealing one step at a time, you must stay in constant communication with God. Since it is always God's fervent wish that you be close to him, letting you see only enough light for the next step keeps you by his side. Your trust makes God happy and ultimately causes you to be more successful and fulfilled.

You may find that your present livelihood can be carried on concurrently with the use of your spiritual gifts, or that your natural talents have already led you into a career or activities that make use of your spiritual gifts. My situation is a good example. As an inspirational writer and an artist I am able to use my talents in my career, but the common thread that runs through everything I do is encouragement and inspiration. One of my gifts is to encourage and uplift others. I also have experienced other gifts at certain times, depending on my situation. The bottom line is that God's gifts improve your life and your gifts often show you the way he is leading you.

If you have made it clear to God that you want his plans and his best for your life, and you still cannot discern what spiritual gifts he has given you, there may be a reason that these things are not coming clear to you. I don't know any other way to say this, but the fact is that you may have to clean up your act. If you are saying that you want God's best for your life, yet you still hold a grudge against someone, or your nurse resentment or bitterness toward someone who has wronged you in the past, you have to get rid of that junk. If you say you want God's will in your life, yet stubbornly insist on your own, you force God to sit back and wait until you get out of your own way. The Holy Spirit will have a hard time getting through to you if your receiver is full of sludge. God wants us to be free and clean, inside and out, which can only happen by living according to his mandates. It only stands to reason that you can't keep doing your own thing while telling God that you want to do his thing. If you are not sure where you are missing it, get alone with God and ask him. He will show you the problem area in your life and help you set things straight.

There are a few other points we need to look at now regarding spiritual gifts. The Bible urges us to desire eagerly and ask for spiritual gifts, so don't be afraid to ask God for the gifts that hold the most appeal for you. Chances are these are the gifts that God wants you to have anyway, but don't be surprised to find that God has also given you a gift that you didn't anticipate. You can be assured that whatever gifts you have, when you use them they will be of benefit to everyone, including you.

Without spiritual gifts, your life as a believer in Jesus lacks power. Without power, you may end up just going through the motions of religion. There is no power to change your life or affect your environment for good if you are just going through motions or acting out traditions. Though some of these things offer some comfort because they are familiar, they lack the power we need to create change in the natural world or the world of the spirit.

Paying attention to our spiritual gifts and using them for others makes us stronger in our faith. When we do not utilize our spiritual gifts, we may end up doing things we are not called to do or have not been given the power to do, which can result in personal shipwreck. Spiritual gifts are indicators of our calling by God, so to act outside of your gifts can be demoralizing and discouraging. For this reason alone, we should try to take the time to find out what gifts God has placed at our disposal and concentrate on developing them. When God reveals your gifts to you, by all means, follow hard after them. Cultivate them and use them and you will continually grow stronger in the power of

God.

Having the Holy Spirit working in us through spiritual gifts allows us to have supernatural power and results. Just as hoping for healing is not the same as having and applying faith for healing, trying to accomplish the work of the Spirit without the power of the Spirit means settling for far less than is available to us. We are all aware that there will be times when we must take aim and fight against the presence or the work of evil in our lives. To undertake such a cause using only our own natural power or ability would be foolhardy, but to use the supernatural power of the Holy Spirit is to take aim and fire with real, effective ammunition.

I mentioned earlier that the presence of evil in the earth has one main aim, which is mankind's downfall and defeat. He will try to bring each of us down in whatever devious way he can. As you grow in the knowledge of God and his ways, you will begin to recognize more and more easily the trouble that the evil one is trying to wreak in your life. But you must have the power of the Holy Spirit to oppose these evils in your life. Do not try to face this enemy under your own steam. That would be like going into battle with no weapons.

To live a life of power you must take the step of being filled with the power of the Holy Spirit. This step differs slightly from just choosing to be a believer in Jesus Christ. When you choose to become a believer, you come under God's protection and guidance and are part of the family of God. But you must also acknowledge the spiritual power of the Holy Spirit and invite him to take up permanent residence in your life. When you do, he is able to use his power on your behalf. You will sense spiritual gifts begin to flow. You may find that your thoughts and opinions about certain subjects suddenly or gradually begin to change. It is impossible for me to name what these may be for you as everyone is so different, but you will notice when changes happen.

For example, I knew a woman who was a dedicated smoker. She enjoyed smoking cigarettes and had no intention of ever stopping in spite of the obvious health risks. However, once she gave her life over to the Holy Spirit, she told me that she was reading her Bible one evening while smoking a cigarette and it suddenly struck her how ridiculous it was that she was smoking and thinking about God at the same time. She realized that her body and spirit now housed the Holy Spirit and she was filling it with smoke and toxins. When this realization hit her, all desire to smoke left her instantly. She butted out that cigarette right then and never smoked again. She suffered no withdrawal symptoms and had no craving to smoke again. Suddenly and without pre-amble, she had become a changed person, a non-smoker.

This is the kind of thing that happens under the power of the Holy Spirit. As you submit yourself to him, he will change your desires so that they please God. It can be truly effortless. Things that mattered before cease to matter and things that you may never have considered before suddenly hold great interest. The power of God is a wonderful thing.

Another experience you may have when you decide to let the Holy Spirit live in you is that you may find sometime when you are talking to God that odd syllables and unknown phrases come to your mind. This is most usual when you actively seek to have more of the Holy Spirit's power or when you are in deep prayer or profound gratitude. This is the gift of speaking in tongues. On the other hand, if you want this gift of speaking in tongues, all you have to do is ask God for it and he will bless you with it.

When I was seventeen years old I made the choice to allow the Holy Spirit to fill my spirit. I had attended a meeting held in a town where I had a summer job. A speaker had come to hold a few informal meetings and I went along with a new friend whom I had met a few weeks previously. Though I had been a believer for many years, learning that I could invite the power of the Holy Spirit into my life was something new to me, but my new friend assured me that she had done it, that it was harmless and in fact, an exciting experience, so I went for it. I remember that I said something simple like, "Holy Spirit please come into my life," and suddenly I found peculiar words pop into my mind. My friend urged me to say them out loud and when I did, more words came out. Suddenly, I was speaking in an unknown language and it seemed as normal as tying my shoes, except that I did not understand what I was saying. Accompanying this experience came a rush of joy and happiness like nothing I'd ever known that bubbled up from somewhere inside me and washed over me. When I went home that night I felt like I was walking on air.

The main purpose of speaking or praying in tongues is that your spirit does the talking without the aid of your conscious mind. The Bible says that doing this builds up or strengthens your spirit. I have found that praying in tongues has enabled me to hear the voice of God much better. It is as though it clears the debris and interference from the channels connecting you with God, allowing his voice to come through with more clarity. Simply put, the more you speak or pray in tongues, the easier it is to hear God.

When you speak in tongues it is the same as speaking with your own language in that you have complete control over when or if you do it. God will not force you to do anything, since force or coercion is just not his style. And as being able to speak in other tongues is one of the spiritual *gifts*, it is completely at your disposal to use or not. In the same way you can't force your mother to wear the sweater you gave her for Christmas last year, God will not force you to avail yourself of his gifts. However, as with any wonderful gift, if you don't use it, it will lie dormant within you and not do you any good. But if you use it, you will experience the joy of seeing the Holy Spirit work in your life and for your benefit.

Finally, I want to talk about the still small voice that God uses to speak to us.

As I mentioned before, I have a room in my house that became vacant when one of my daughters left home. (It's okay. She grew up first.) I call it my sewing room, my husband calls it his den, and our guests call it the guest room. In it we have a futon that converts into a sofa and when I sit on it I have a spectacular view of a magnificent snow-capped mountain. It is a rare summer when all of the snow melts away, and it usually leaves a patch on the side facing me that is shaped like an angel. The surrounding mountains are covered in lush ever-green forests. This is where I like to go to talk to God.

I live in a quiet little town and I love the silence we enjoy. Though the train goes through town several times a day, and we hear an occasional siren (weekly, not daily, and usually only on long weekends), most mornings are so silent all I hear is the clock ticking or a bird outside my window greeting the day. It is in these quiet times and in this quiet place where I go regularly to talk with God.

Find that quiet place where you can be alone and uninterrupted for a length of time, perhaps a half hour to an hour or more. I usually take with me a journal or notebook and a pen that writes easily and is comfortable to use. You can begin by talking to God as though he were in the room with you. Don't be concerned if you feel silly or feel like you are talking to yourself. If it helps, close your eyes and imagine that God is in the room with you. If it helps you, you might imagine a light, a candle flame, or an image of Jesus you may have seen from artwork, but this serves solely as a focus to calm your thoughts. If you are not comfortable with this idea, then feel free to not use it. Something else will work just as well for you.

Remember, as I said earlier, that it is important just to be yourself. You can talk to God in the same way you would talk to a friend. A good place to begin is to thank him. I like to thank God for the things that are going well for me, such as my health or a good night's sleep. When I focus on the things that I have to be thankful for, it enables me to see how God has been working on my behalf. Even though sometimes troubles loom large, by deliberately focusing on the positive I find that God's peace begins to take over my mind. Tensions float away and everything looks better from the vantage point of thankfulness.

I am thankful for a warm home on a cold day, the fact that my winter coat will last another year, I have enough money to pay this month's bills, and for peace of mind. I am grateful that when I ask God for harmony in my marriage, my husband and I get along better. I am thankful that I own a reliable car, get to work alone, have beautiful views all around me, and have low-stress. The list of things that we can be thankful for is endless and as you cultivate a thankful spirit, the Holy Spirit becomes more and more comfortable in you and you will more easily see God's hand at work in your days.

This quiet time with God is the time to bring up your concerns and requests. Is there anything bothering you today? Talk to God about it. Do you have a problem at home for which you have no clear answer? Are you under pressure, stressed out, or over-scheduled, yet can't seem to find a way to lighten your load? He can help you to find clarity about what is most important. Do you have a difficult situation at work or in your business for which you need help, but have no one to whom you can turn?

God is not only interested in helping you, he is endowed with the ability to do so, and he can equip you with whatever you need to see you through. Not only that, but he sees what you cannot see, such as the problems others are facing that affect you, or what your real fears are. Bring these all up before God and ask for his help. You may not understand how things can work out, but God knows, and as you give him permission to work in your life, he can straighten out the most tangled situation and undertake measures that will change things in ways you never imagined.

As you talk to God, ask questions and be specific. If you need an answer, be quiet long enough for him to reply to you. Sometimes you will hear silence, in which case, just trust that God has things under control. Just relinquish your problems into God's hands for him to be allowed to work on your behalf. This is where trust comes in. As you trust God more and more with your problems and plan, he can do more and more to help you succeed.

When something comes into your mind, you may want to jot it down in your journal. Don't feel that it has to be something huge or profound to count. Sometimes all you need is just one word or two, so that is all he will give you. Other times he "dictates" pages of commentary and you will have to write fast to keep up. This is what most often happens with me. As I have grown to know God's voice, what he tells me in my quiet sessions with him is often long and detailed. I have several journals that over the years I have filled with his messages to me. The parts of this course that are shown in bold are taken from my journals and I have included them for your benefit and edification. You can see that when you take the time to seek God and listen to him, he is very open to talk with you about all sorts of things. I have not included a lot of material from my journals because it is too personal, but some of what God has spoken to me over the years is valuable for anyone.

You may understand immediately what is said or what it means, or not. If you do, it could be the answer that you seek to whatever problem or issue you have brought before God. It may be something you've known all along, or an idea that is totally new to you. Sometimes only one word will occur to you, or a phrase, or perhaps someone's face or name will pop into your mind. If this happens, you may experience an urge to contact this person in some way.

If you are confused about what to do in your particular situation, don't be afraid to ask God for more information and wait for an answer. God won't do the work for us but he will definitely help us if we need help. He is not a hard taskmaster. I have found over the years that I know when God speaks to me because he says things that I had not thought of on my own. His ideas are sometimes quite different from mine. If I have puzzled with a problem for a while and not come up with a solution, God will often provide me the answer that has eluded me.

If you know what God is telling you to do, then it is your responsibility to act on that knowledge. Perhaps you need to forgive someone before you can move forward. Maybe someone needs your help, but you have been dragging your feet about going to them. If the answer to your problem has been in the back of your mind for a while and becomes more pronounced as you seek God's input, then you already know what it is you are to do.

You may also have a prior experience come to your mind that holds some information that will help you through your day or your problem. Very often our problems are ones that we have faced before. Prior experiences sometimes hold the key to answers for the present.

If you know what to do but don't *want* to do it, ask yourself what is stopping you from obeying the urgings of the Holy Spirit. Keep in mind that whatever God suggests or recommends to you is for your own good. That means it will ultimately improve your life in some way even if you are unable to see how just now.

Sometimes when you are talking to God and asking for answers, it feels like you are the only one talking. This doesn't mean that God is ignoring you or is too busy with someone else who has bigger issues to deal with than you do. It may mean you are not ready to hear the answer, or that God will reveal it to you in a way other than directly hearing his voice.

Recently, I had a problem that had nagged me for some time. I knew there was an impediment to moving forward, and I knew that the issue centred on another person whom I know, but I could never seem to put my finger on the real cause of the problem. I had spoken to God about it numerous times and left it with him, but as time went on, the realization that I could not move forward until this issue was resolved became clearer and more insistent. It felt like I was circling around the real source of trouble yet I remained unable to find the solution. One day I told God that I had to find the answer. I was not hearing it directly from him, and when I spoke to him he always seemed to want to address other topics. I'm not sure why, perhaps it didn't matter just then, but I needed a breakthrough and the frustration I felt was pushing me toward a snapping point. I needed to know where the problem lay.

Then one night, just before waking, I had a clear and vivid dream about this person. In the dream I saw this person act in certain ways followed by my response to the behaviour. If I did something which I had been planning to do in my waking life, this person reacted a certain way. In the dream, I was so disturbed about this behaviour that I had to go to great lengths to restore equilibrium in the relationship. After I woke up, the images from this dream kept running through my mind. I began to see that I had a fear that if I were to persist in my plans, this other person would cause me a great deal of pain and suffering. This subconscious belief had been preventing me from doing the very things that I felt God was leading me to do. As I couldn't see it in my waking hours, God used my dreams to bring the issue to my attention.

Once I had clarity about this fear, I went to the other person and shared my concerns. What I learned was that what I feared was just a fear and had no basis in reality or with the other's behaviour or intentions. God set me free from that hidden fear, granting me the liberty to carry out his plans and my desires.

Now, you may be one who cries, "How do I know I can trust God? What if things don't work out? What if I make a mistake?"

These are all good questions, ones that I struggled with for many years. My mind said, *how can I trust God when I don't know if he's trustworthy?* What I found was that the less I chose to trust God with my problems and trials, the less he was able to work. Because I was unsure of his reliability, I would pray in a half-hearted manner, with hope rather than with faith, then try to work things out myself just in case God didn't come through for me. What changed it all for me was finding some teaching that trained me to think in a different way.

I learned that I had to make a *conscious choice* to relinquish my cares to God in spite of my fears. As long as I held on and worried over the problem, he was not able to perform anything on my behalf. As I let go, he began to work. It took a long time to be able to loosen my grip on every area of my life and allow God to have things done his way. To be honest, I still sometimes have to remind myself that God is there for me. But experience has taught me that when I choose to give my issues to God to look after, my life is so much easier and so much more peaceful. It becomes a stress-free existence because I know that God is in control, he can handle my problems as I hand them over to him, and I can go on just doing whatever he tells me to do each day.

I'm bringing you into a place you've never been before. It is a place of trusting me like you've never trusted me before. You will find as you seek me that anxieties that have plagued you all your life will begin to drop away from you. You will change in your thinking without even realizing it. You will just wake up one day and realize that things that have been a problem for you all of your life have just gotten up and left and you are bothered no more.

I can do this. I can change you in the blink of an eye when you are yielded to me. That image you have of continual softening toward me and my will and desire for you is the image I want you to keep in mind. Move from pillow to marshmallow to vapour – soft, soft, soft. The softer you are toward me, the greater impression I make on your life. This is how you become conformed to my image.

Please try to spend time with me every day. In this time I will speak to you and guide you into what I want you to do. I will show you how to proceed step by step.

I am sometimes guilty of hearing one thing, then taking off after it like a hound after a hare, only to realize way down the road that I took a wrong turn and ended up where I didn't want to be, and nowhere near where God had intended for me. I didn't get the whole set of instructions before filling in the blanks.

As a creative person, I always have a lot of ideas, most of which I think are great when they first come to me. I get very excited about new ideas and plans, and leap into action trying to bring them into fruition. Patiently waiting for more information from God has not always been my strong point.

But after a few experiences that have left me holding a bag of broken dreams, I have learned that just because an idea occurs to me doesn't mean it came from God and doesn't mean that I need to do something with it. I have discovered that before I act on my next fantastic idea, I need to wait until I get a definite answer and, if need be, the next step. When I have done this, I am happy to say that God has warned me away from some things that would have ended in disaster or perhaps just in an unhappy situation. Too often I have only taken time to discuss my plans with God after they have started to go wrong. While this is better than not discussing them with him at all, it doesn't hold a candle to starting out with God's plans firmly in my hands.

Let me give you an example. I used to have a wholesale business in which I produce several lines of stationery products that sold in the gift market. While operating that business, I had the idea that since the hobby of scrapbooking had become so popular it would be smart to design and create a product line for this market. So, without first consulting with my senior partner, God, I went ahead and spent many hours creating designs and themes and concepts to sell to scrapbooking stores. Since the product designs required painting, I sourced paints and brushes to sell, and created labels for the paint jars to coordinate with the product line. Then I registered to exhibit at a big scrapbooking wholesale trade show being held in Las Vegas. I was sure that this show would launch my scrapbooking line and, of course, make me a lot of money.

Hours of work went into creating a booth that was beautiful and portable. I hired a staff member to help with the preparations for the show which included creating sample scrapbooks for promotional material, new price lists and order forms, signage, table covers, display units, back-drops, finding and purchasing proper lighting, and dealing with all the other little details that are required to exhibit successfully at a trade show. I enlisted the help and paid the expenses of another person to attend the show with me to assist with the set up, staffing the booth, handling orders, selling, and transporting my products and equipment.

By the time I was ready to leave for the show I was completely exhausted. If you have ever exhibited at a trade show, you know how tiring it can be. When I arrived at the show I discovered that the booth I had been assigned had been misrepresented and rather than being placed in a busy thoroughfare leading to a restaurant as was suggested in the show guides, my booth was in a narrow hallway leading to nowhere. The show was poorly attended, and the bulk of the traffic bypassed the hallway where my booth was located without so much as a turn of the head. My product received some interest but no buyers, and by the third day of this four-day show, I was so worn out that I no longer cared. I just wanted to soak my sore feet and go to bed for a long time.

When I got back home, and after I had rested up, I sat down one day to talk this over with God. He is so kind. He didn't once berate me or tell me he could have told me so, or any other such admonishment. What he told me was that even if that product had been successful, I would not like where it would take me. If I had made lots of sales and tons of money, I would not have been happy doing that business anyway. He knew that all along. I could have saved myself a whole lot of time, effort, and money had I only consulted God in the first place.

In another instance, I did consult him on something that I thought was a great opportunity. He gave me permission to pursue it, but warned me about the way it would affect my life, and what to watch out for. He told me that if I was not careful about certain things, I would face unpleasant consequences and detailed what I could expect. The warning helped me immensely as I found that when I was not careful, I indeed experienced exactly what he had said, but since I recognized it the minute it happened, I was able to rectify the situation immediately rather than discover my problem months or years down the road.

It is hard to imagine a stress-free life in today's busy world, but walking hand in hand with God will give you that. When you can cast your cares over upon him, knowing that he cares so much for you, your life will take on a peace that really does defy understanding. In the midst of chaos all around you, God will be there with you, hold you up when you are weak, nudge you forward when you need a boost, be the answer to your prayers and problems, give you comfort when you suffer, and love you with a love beyond anything you will ever experience. To know him is to love him and to be loved by him. Such a great gift knows no equal.

Journal

God gives each of his children spiritual gifts to help us through life, to give us direction, and to help others with whom we come into contact. When you read through the list of spiritual gifts itemized in this chapter, do any seem to be a 'fit' for you? What are they?

In addition to spiritual gifts, God gives each of us special talents and abilities that suit our personalities. Which abilities on this list can you identify as being most like you? Are you comfortable, knowing that these are your God-given gifts? Why or why not?

When you recognize and accept the gifts that God has placed within you, your life may change direction. As you contemplate the gifts God has given you, can you see how your life may change, or does this knowledge confirm that you are perfectly placed to maximize your gifts?

If you were to ask God right now how you might use your gifts in greater measure, what do you sense he is telling you?

We are to earnestly desire spiritual gifts, and ask for ones we would like to have. What gifts would you like to see developed in yourself that you don't feel that you currently have? Why?

Remember that the gifts that hold the most appeal to us are usually the gifts God wants us to develop. As you seek to receive special gifts, how do you feel about these choices in relation to God's plans for your life?

Without the spiritual gifts God has for us, we lack the spiritual power to bring about God's will in the earth. Without power, we can just go through the motions of lifeless religious or spiritual rituals without affecting any significant change in our own lives or the world around us. How do you feel about this contrast of a spiritual life with the power provided by our spiritual gifts, and a life of ritual or practice without power? Explain.

By not accessing the spiritual gifts that God has provided for us, we settle for much less than he has made available to us. The power of the Holy Spirit is on hand to help us use our gifts. Explain how you could use more of God's power in your life.

To move deeper into the things of the Spirit, we must take a step in addition to becoming a believer. That step entails inviting the Holy Spirit to take up residence in your soul. Accomplishing this is simple and will change your life like nothing else. By repeating the following unpretentious prayer, you can invite the Holy Spirit into your life. This step is also called the baptism of the spirit. Say aloud, "Holy Spirit, please come into my life now and do whatever work that needs to be done to fill me with your Spirit, power and ability." Now, what usually happens is a surge or rush of joy and profound happiness. As you enjoy this feeling of connection and perhaps euphoria you may begin to notice words or sounds entering your mind. The Holy Spirit wants to give you a special language to pray with that allows your spirit to speak directly to God's Spirit without having to first travel through your mind. As you speak aloud the syllables or words that you hear in your mind, your own spiritual language will emerge. Go ahead and do that now. This is an experience you don't want to miss out on. If you feel like it, write about this experience now.

Speaking in your spiritual language, also known as speaking in tongues, accomplishes several purposes. It is the evidence that you have been filled with the Holy Spirit. Speaking in tongues builds up or re-charges your spirit. When you speak to God in tongues, you are talking to him in his own language. No one will understand you since the language you are using is heaven's language. When you speak or pray in tongues, the Holy Spirit reveals the mysteries of the spirit to you. Speaking in tongues also builds and strengthens your faith. Now that you can speak in tongues, you will find that doing so brings great comfort to your soul. Explain your new experience feels here.

God often speaks with us in a still, small voice. In the stillness of your soul, you can hear him talk to you. As you practice spending time with God and listening for his quiet voice the easier it becomes to hear him no matter what your situation. Take some time to talk and listen to God now and record what you hear.

Do you have any problems right now for which you want or need God's help? What are they? When you ask for God's input, what is he saying to you?

Some people have difficulty trusting God because they do not have an accurate picture of what God is like. In this space, write down everything good you can think of, every attribute that is wonderful or lovely, then write that this is what God is like. If you want a description, see 1 Corinthians 13: 4-8.

When you hear God speak to you, it's important to let him finish before you begin to do what he has told you. How do you think knowing this will affect your experience of hearing and complying with his leading.

It is difficult for many of us to imagine a stress-free life, yet Jesus promises that he will never ask us to bear more than we are able. I believe that as we become more in tune with God's plans for us, our lives will become more serene and happy. If God were to give you the desires of your heart, do you think that your life would have less stress? Why?

EIGHT

Dedicating Your Life

At the beginning of each year I like to take time to look back at the past year and review the goals and plans I made a year ago. I take some time to evaluate what I had then planned to do, and see how it all worked out. By reading the notes I kept throughout the year, I can see where I made changes along the way, where I decided to discard some plans completely, and where I accomplished what I had set out to do.

For the latter part of last year, I experienced a change in direction for my business ventures and my life. One does not create a business in a vacuum, and most entrepreneurs will tell you that they "live" their business, at least in the start-up and growth phases. As I evaluated where I had been and what I'd done during the year, I tried to create new plans and goals for the coming year. I knew that some things needed to change, but I was not sure how I should change them or what I needed to do to create different outcomes. I had been finding it difficult to put a finger on the exact direction I should take, and what I should do next.

In this personal climate of uncertainty, I sat down in my reading room one afternoon to see what the Lord had to say about what I was to do next. Because of the rush and busyness of the Christmas holiday season, with all the activity required to help create a happy time for my family, I had not taken much time to be alone with God and absorb his peace. I felt out of touch with him and out of sorts with myself. I was finding it difficult even to concentrate on the questions whirling about in my distracted mind.

When I managed to get still enough to hear the voice of the Holy Spirit, it seemed to me that, though a couple of my questions had been answered, I still had no clear direction about the next steps to take in my businesses and my personal life. After talking to God and waiting for nearly an hour to get clear directions from him and hearing nothing, I finally I put my journal away, got up and went back to work.

When you run a business or have a job, manage a family and a home, and deal with a social life, it seems like there is always something that demands your attention, always one more thing to be done. Sometimes it is difficult to stop thinking long enough about all the demands that crowd in and claim your attention to be able to concentrate on becoming still and quiet before God. Yet I find that no matter how busy, distracted or overwhelmed I am, God knows exactly what is going on with me and understands precisely what I need and why I need it.

I finished that day by working on a large project that had been taking me a long time to complete. I had left my quiet time without a satisfactory answer to my inquiries, but God and I both knew that I was trying too hard and was too distracted by outside demands for me to hear easily, so he waited until I stopped thinking about it, then presented me with what he knew I needed to hear.

The answer to my biggest question, "what next?", came in a couple of ways. First, I received an installment of an email newsletter to which I subscribe. The message was about setting goals for the coming year. *How timely*, I thought as I read the text. To my surprise, the author claimed that he had stopped setting goals about what to do and had changed the question to ask, "Who would I like to be this year?"

This is a much different question than, "What do I want to do?" It instantly changes your perspective from one of accomplishing or achieving something you don't currently have or haven't done to, "Who will you be regardless of anything else?"

I believe that the question at the heart of this, and at the heart of life's biggest question of all, is, "What am I here for?" or "What is the purpose of my life in the first place?"

I believe that God created each one of us to be an individual, like no one else. Since it is indisputable that no two of us are exactly alike, presumably we were each created to be completely unique for a reason. God is interested in you being just you. Let's assume that your main life purpose was to be the most *you* possible. How would you behave as the best possible version of yourself? Are you trying to be something that you're not? God has placed in you a picture of yourself at your best. What does it look like?

As I sought and waited for clear answers, I began to take a look at that picture; that dream, of what I could be if I were being my best.

The second part of the answer to came as I was getting my breakfast. (It seems to me that the Lord often speaks to me when I am involved in the most mundane tasks making the bed, driving, doing laundry, or cleaning up around the house.) My questions had been on my mind for several days as I waited for some answers to sift out. This time God spoke as I was setting the table. By now, my mind had become unoccupied enough to hear him speak. As I set out my cereal, I heard these words in my thoughts: "Use your talents, not your abilities."

I knew that God had spoken to me. He says things that I would never have thought of myself. What he says usually stands in stark contrast to the surrounding stream of thoughts flowing through my mind. I had been trying to figure out something else entirely, like whether to advertise, or to create some new designs or other task-related project.

He knew that I needed to have a major purpose statement against which to measure everything I am tempted to do. I often find it difficult to decide where I should best spend my time, energy, and money. Since, like most of us, I have the ability to do many things, it is often difficult to settle on what would be the optimal course of action.

Now just because God told me to use my talents, not my abilities, doesn't mean this is what he is saying to you. He may want you to concentrate on something entirely different (although I believe that he always wants us to use the talents that he gave us). Don't follow what others say you should do, have or be. God created you as an individual and has a particular plan in mind for you that suits you better than anything else, and better than it would suit anyone else.

I give talents to make it obvious to people what they are called to do. The world messes it all up because the enemy of your soul perverts everything that is good and true. Don't follow the dictates of the world regarding how you should spend your time earning your living. Follow your heart, for that is where I have placed the truth for you. Do what you yearn to do but for whatever reason feel you can't or are afraid to do. Follow those yearnings. Keep the main issue continually before your eyes. Concentrate on that one work and push all else to the side. Don't be pulled away from your heart's desire. Don't allow other things to distract you. Put on blinders and look straight ahead. Focus on your heart's work and don't look to the right or the left.

Make a plan, set your goal, do the work step by step. This is how you arrive. There is no other way. The work will not get done unless you do it. So do it. It will be worth it. You will find not only fulfillment but also joy, prosperity, health and love. Don't hesitate. Today is the day to begin.

However, just because you *can* do something doesn't mean you *should* do it. For example, I am quite capable of creating a gourmet meal for twenty people if I had to but that does not mean I should become a caterer. The fact that I'm able to drive does not indicate a career as a truck driver or taxi driver. Having the ability to do something does not mean that it is necessarily the right choice for you. That's why it is vital we use our talents instead.

That morning not long ago God spoke to me in those very certain terms how to live, succeed and prosper. Before I go any further, I want to deal with the subject of obedience. I can imagine that many of you reading these words or listening to the recordings of this text may want to gag at the thought of obeying anyone, even God himself. Our modern western culture is strong on individualism, independence, and self-reliance, and short on being a follower. Except perhaps in military situations, obedience is something that doesn't get talked about much. Your boss may ask you to do a job, expecting compliance, and rightly so, but if he or she came to you and demanded that you obey his or her commands, you might be tempted to give that boss a quick pop in the nose, grab your coat and head out the door.

Or maybe you wouldn't do something that rash. Instead you would gripe behind the boss' back, grudgingly performing the required task while resenting being told what to do. Maybe your attitude would interfere with your performance of the tasks at hand, and sooner or later, one way or another, you would make sure to get out from under that boss' command.

Obedience means adapting your own will to that of another. It means submitting to authority, and complying with the commands or instructions of that person over us. We can do it willingly, we can do it kicking and screaming, or we can refuse to do it altogether. How we see the act of obedience makes all the difference.

So let's look at obedience from the following point of view. Suppose that you have the opportunity to work under someone whose handiwork you have long admired. The chance to work with this person is a "dream come true" for you, since you know that what you will learn during your time with him or her will be invaluable to your future success and happiness. This person knows so much more than you do about your field of work that just being around him or her will change your life and career in so many wonderful ways. You would leap at the chance to obey, no matter what it was called.

As an artist, I shall use myself as an illustration. Suppose I had the opportunity to go to Italy and study for a week-long workshop under none other than the famous grand master, Leonardo da Vinci. (I know he's dead, but let's pretend.) I would make all my travel arrangements, reserve my accommodations and arrive on the appointed day ready to meet the master himself. I would have shopped carefully from the supply list given to me after registering for the workshop and would have purchased the exact supplies required to use for the projects to be assigned that week. I would want to arrive early on the first day to make sure that I found parking nearby then located the right studio so I could get a good seat for the class. When the master artist arrived, my attention would be on nothing else. After all, learning from this great man would be the opportunity of a lifetime.

On the morning of the first day of the class I am ready, sitting in my place with all my materials and supplies set out. Suddenly, Signor Da Vinci strides into the studio, his shoes crusted with the dust of Carrera marble, and his fingers coloured by pigments and charcoal. His tutorial begins. He demonstrates for the class the techniques that, history has proven, make him one of the greatest artistic masters of all time. I listen intently to his every directive and make careful notes as he speaks and reveals his centuries-old secrets. When it is time for the students to put into practise what he has just demonstrated, we begin to paint and he strolls around the studio, checking each student's work. Suddenly, he is at my elbow.

"Do it like this," he instructs. Taking the paintbrush from my hand and, with a few deft, precise strokes, he shows me how to improve my work, save me a great deal of time creating paintings, and dramatically increase the value of my art. He smiles as he hands my brush back to me, then moves on to talk with another student. My eyes follow him as he strolls away. Should I obey, or should I pay no attention to the instructions of this master?

You must agree that it makes no sense for me to disregard his instructions. How foolish it would be to get all worked up, fuming, "Just who does he think he is, telling me what to do? I'm just as good an artist as he is!" Even if I were not to react with anger at his direction, it would still be irrational not to obey. When I understand that the person whose instructions I have sought is infinitely more capable, knowl-edgeable, and wise than I am, in any area of artistic endeavour, it shows good judgment to follow his lead, doesn't it?

Dedicating yourself to following God's purpose and obeying his leading is easy once you recognize that God's plan offers you the best of all possible options. When you understand that God knows what is best for you as an individual and also for those whose lives you share, and he always has your best interests at heart, it takes the guesswork out of whether to follow his leading. It simply requires that we trust God and trust ourselves to sense his leading and to follow his direc-tion.

This brings us to another important issue – trust. How do you dedicate yourself to following an unseen God? How do you trust your-self to know that you have heard his voice?

As in any relationship, the more time you spend getting to know God, the easier it becomes to trust him. We have discussed in previous chapters how to spend more time in the presence of God to hear and know his voice speaking to you. We all must make the decision to trust him by choice. Stick your toe in the water and see what happens. Jump! You can only learn to trust by trusting. At some point we all need to dive in and go for it.

By dedicating yourself to following the Spirit, a whole new vista of possibilities and opportunities opens up before you. You might find that your life takes a sudden change of direction once you know what God is calling you to do. You may find that the dreams you have had since childhood seem suddenly possible, and that God will show you how they can be achieved. Perhaps you will discover that what you thought you should be doing no longer has any appeal and that you are drawn to other new experiences you had never before considered tackling.

Did you know that the Bible says that God gives us the desires of our hearts? This beautiful statement can be taken two ways. First, he puts his desires in us to go after what he knows will make us happy. Then, he goes about helping us to attain the desires that we yearn to have fulfilled. So if you long to use your most cherished talents and abilities, God can help you do that. He wants you to use the gifts he placed in you and will help you be the best you can be.

Do you think that dedicating your life to following God's leading sounds like a tough call? What is difficult is choosing his will over your own. But once you make the decision to seek God, you will need some guidance and support for your journey.

So let's look at this from the perspective of a traveller.

Suppose that you are planning the vacation of a lifetime. Perhaps it is a cruise around the world, a European tour, or a month on a beautiful tropical island. You are finally able to afford this dream vacation and everything has fallen into place for you to get away for the required time. Your work situation now allows for you to take the time off that you need, or perhaps you just retired and the trip you have long saved for is now possible.

This kind of trip is going to require planning, isn't it? You will have to choose your travelling companions, if there are to be any, and pick a destination or itinerary. You need a list so you don't forget any of the equally vital steps in planning your venture. You'll have to speak to a travel agent, research your options, get pricing and choose a departure date and location. Once you have completed all of the items on your list, there will be preparations to make prior to leaving.

And you will have to make another list or two - find someone to take your dog, if you have one, or water your plants, or keep an eye on your house while you are gone. Then you must shop for the right clothes to wear on your trip. If you are taking a cruise, you will need beach wear, outdoor wear, evening wear and casual outfits, all to suit the climate. If you are flying into a different season, you'll shop and pack accordingly. If your plan includes hiking in the Alps or scuba-diving in the Caribbean, there is all your gear to get ready before you go.

Then you will check your luggage and make sure you have the right bags. They must suit your travelling situation and your own physical strength, stand up to the wear and tear of airport carousels, baggage handlers, and sidewalks, and also be the right size to hold all your stuff.

Now, let me ask you, will you have any trouble dedicating yourself to doing all these things in preparation for a wonderful time? Will you agonize over whether or not to pack your flippers and snorkel so you can dive the reefs? Would you neglect to investigate climate conditions, visa requirements, medical issues, or the political situation in your destination country? Would you refuse to think about booking your cruise, yet still expect to get on the ship when it comes into port? Of course you wouldn't do any of these things.

No, your anticipation of wonderful future experiences would wipe away any anxiety or difficulty you might have about how everything will work out. You know that with the proper planning, even if things don't go exactly as anticipated, you will still have a fabulous time and be able to enjoy the memories you make for the rest of your life. Dedication to the cause is not a problem, is it?

God's plans for you are always accompanied with a big "yes!" from him. He says that the plans he has for you are for good and not for evil, to give you a future and a hope of more good to come.

Look at these words of the Lord from my journal written several years ago:

It is my purpose that my children live in peace, in joy and in fulfilment. The abundant life I have provided for you is yours for the taking when you abide (dwell, stay) in me.

Listen to the call of your heart for it is here that I speak to you. Follow the yearnings that groan within you, for this is my spirit propelling you, calling you, pulling you. Do not be drawn away from the course on which I have put you. Do not allow circumstances to turn your ear, turn your attentions away from that to which I have called you. Stay true to the voice of your heart for out of it flows the abundance that I give. Do not be sidetracked by trouble, circumstances and issues of life, for I have made you and called you to a special thing. Stay true and experience the joy that I have promised to those who are obedient to my voice.

Dedication requires that we make a definite and determined decision. It means that you set your face like flint to follow a particular path or course of action no matter how things look at the start or how many obstacles you encounter along the way. Dedication requires commitment, resolve and perseverance. It is not for the wishy-washy.

In order to succeed in hearing the voice of the Spirit, we must trust and obey. I know that concept sounds old-fashioned in our instant, microwave world. We want to do things ourselves, get it done fast, and go home and watch television. While there is nothing wrong with any of these things per se, we will miss out on many adventures and thrills-of-a-lifetime if we fail to make the choice to dedicate ourselves to the life of the Spirit.

Living with God's design imprinted on your heart and pulsing through your thoughts gives richness and intention to everything that you do. With an overriding vision of God's purpose before you, much of life's complexity becomes simple.

Having said that, the one sole purpose we all share is to know and love God and show love to others. If you do nothing else but love God and show your love to others your entire life, you can call yourself a success. You will have fulfilled the commands of Jesus. That's because when you love God with all your heart and love others like you would want to be loved, God will open all kinds of doors for you to live the life of your dreams.

But wait, what if you slip up, yell at your kids, say nasty things about your boss? Easy. Ask forgiveness and pick up where you left off. In everything the Holy Spirit is your helper. You can ask for help to accomplish whatever you are called to do, or that you have set your intention to achieve, as long as it is in line with loving God and loving others.

We have all heard about people who are driven to succeed, or driven to accomplish some lofty goal. When it comes to living your purpose, you can be driven or you can be called.

God does not coerce us, push us or needle us. He calls us. If you feel driven, examine who or what is driving you. The enemy wants you to suffer at his hands and will use whatever tactic he can to control and manipulate you. If you have areas in your life where he can get a toehold, he will deceive you into believing that what you feel driven to do will give you peace and fulfillment. But he is a liar and will see to it that you never have peace and joy.

By contrast, the Holy Spirit draws and sweetly persuades us to follow him. Jesus said, "Here I am! I stand at the door and knock. If anyone hears my voice and opens the door, I will come in and eat with him, and he with me."[1] When we invite him, he comes in with his gentle, engaging Spirit, shares life with us and gives rest to our souls.

Once you have made it your life's mission to love God and love others and allow God to work out his plans for you and through you, you can get on with the more specific aspects of how God wants you to use your life. What is it that God is calling you to do, be or have?

God uses the desires of our hearts to lead us to what he has planned for our lives.

With that in mind, there are other clues that he uses to help us to follow his leading. We have already examined at some length the spiritual gifts with which God endows us, and how we can use that knowledge to be led by the Holy Spirit.

To take a closer look at your purpose and what God wants for you, ask yourself the following questions:

"What are my core values? What interests draw me? What do I cherish, appreciate, or treasure?" You may be passionate about creativity, adventure, beauty, or compassion. Perhaps you value accuracy, achievement, humour, loyalty, cooperation, or challenge. Admit to yourself what is true for you.

Sometimes we try to form ourselves to fit into the space before us rather than simply being ourselves and seeking out spaces that are made to fit us.

When I was young and living at home with my parents and siblings, we spent the evenings during the long winter months working on jigsaw puzzles. My Dad and I were the most avid jigsaw puzzlers. We would spread out a big one during the Christmas holidays and take turns working on it as the days went by. When it was finished we'd let it sit out for a few days so that we could enjoy our accomplishment before crumpling it up and putting the pieces back in the box. Then we would get another one out of the closet in the hallway and start again.

Sometimes when you are doing a jigsaw puzzle you find a piece that looks like exactly the right one for a space you have. The bumps and curves all seem to line up and the colour seems to be exact. My Dad would hand me that piece that seemed perfect and I would place it in the open spot only to find out that it didn't quite fit. Dad would say, "Ram it, push harder; it has to fit." Of course he was joking and we'd eventually concede that the piece did not fit and keep on hunting for the ideal one. It became a family joke, so that now when something doesn't fit where we think it should, we say, "Ram it."

I think we do that to ourselves sometimes. We try to fit ourselves into shapes and spaces and careers and relationships that really aren't a fit. It looks like it might work out so we ram it. We try to re-mould ourselves to ideals or expectations that are simply not true to our values. And since our values match our personalities and our personalities were designed by God, then adhering to what we truly value lines us up with God's will.

There is nothing that you *should* like or that *should* be important to you because someone says it should, only what you *do* like and *is* important to you. You are okay being just who you are. Ask yourself what group, pursuit, livelihood, or cause would give you the most satisfaction and allow you to live out your core values. What ideas and initiatives attract you or move you? Are you interested in wildlife, children, the elderly or justice? Does your heart go out to single mothers, the unemployed, the disabled or sick, the grieving, or the homeless? Do you have a passion for politics, healthcare issues or business? Ask God to draw you toward your best life and he will show you how to live it.

God once told me that the call of your heart is the heart of your call. Whatever you feel drawn to or find irresistible is most likely what God is urging you to go after. At the heart of what God is calling you to do with your days, what kind of person to be, or what you need to have, is the heart of what you need to go after. God loves it when you follow your heart's desires - the desires that he has placed there - and once you make the decision to follow where God is leading your heart, I believe that all heaven stands up to cheer you on.

When we communicate with God, we can let down our guard and be perfectly ourselves. He wants us to come to him in spirit and in truth. That means that we can be completely open and honest in his presence. Let your spirit lead you and be your most real self.

Dedicating yourself to God's ways means that he will take whatever we offer him and make it better. Even if we blow it again and again we can always return to him. He never fails to take us back, help us up, and set us on our feet again. He starts just where he left off, leading us back to the path of our best possible life. If God had a refrigerator, your picture would be on it.

Life in the Spirit is not a life of drudgery, duty, or penury. It is not one long stretch of suffering or degradation. If you believe that it is, you have been sold a bill of goods. The bad PR folks have turned your head in the wrong direction.

Reject the lies of the enemy and embrace the truth of God's love for you. God loved you so much that he gave his only Son to pay for your own soul, so that you could become one of his favourite kids. All you have to do is accept the gift and throw your lot in with him. Every step may not be easy, but it is a love affair beyond compare, a romance of infinite proportions, and the never-ending thrill of a lifetime. How great and how wonderful is that!

[1]Revelation 3:20 (New Living Translation).

Journal

From time to time it's a good idea for us to step back from our lives and evaluate where we are and where we want to go or what we want to change. As you look at your life today, assess where you have come from in the past year, what you have accomplished, and measure how you are doing. Are you where you want to be? If not, what needs to be different?

God wants to be part of our life planning from the smallest details to the big picture. As you talk with God today, why not ask him what his plan is for your day, or for your year. Write down what you learn.

I mention that God once told me to use my talents not my abilities. I don't expect you to take the same advice since what he said was specifically for me. However, in light of this comment, think of the talents that you may have stopped using or have been pushed aside in favour of using your abilities. How would it feel to use your talents more?

God gives each of us talents and abilities to help us choose the appropriate path in life. List all of your talents that you can think of and how you might be able to use more of them more often.

We need to make plans and set goals for our lives, but it is important to remember to talk to God as we do. He will help us to choose the right goals and will lead us on the right paths. Write down some of your goals and plans here.

God encourages us to become like children in our trust of him. By doing this, we allow him to care for us and help us in life. In what areas of your life could you relinquish control and give it over to God to look after? How does it feel to let go of control?

The concept of obedience is not one that many of us find easy to consider. When you look at obedience from the point of view of being offered the great privilege of following a master, it takes on a different tone. What are your feelings about obeying God? Why do you feel this way?

In order to trust someone we need to feel that he or she is worthy of our trust. We can either make the choice to trust, regardless of our knowledge of God, or we can increase our knowledge of God then choose to trust. What are your thoughts on trusting?

If you have difficulty trusting God, what do you think would have to happen for you to be able to trust?

What will you change to allow that to happen?

In the Bible (Psalm 37:4) it says that when we take delight in God, he will give us the desires of our hearts. What does it mean to you to take delight in God?

When you think about dedicating your life to how God wants you to live, how does that affect you? Do you see that as positive or negative? Why?

God wants us to be whole, healthy and free. In what areas of your life would you like to experience wholeness, health and freedom?

If you view life as a journey and God as your travelling companion and guide, how will you live knowing that he has a wonderful trip planned for you? Does this knowledge change your perspective? How?

God's purpose for us is that we live in peace, joy and fulfillment. In what ways do you think you would like to change to experience more of those in your life?

By dedicating ourselves to a life in the Spirit, we must stay in continual communication with the Spirit. What will you do to be in constant contact with God?

Jesus reduced all the laws of God to only two commandments: love God, and love others. By living with these two tenets guiding you, how do you think your life will change?

God will never drive you to do anything but will lead into your best life. What do feel God has called you or is calling you to do, either just for today or as a life calling?

Do you feel that you are you currently on the path or paths that God has called you to? Express how you feel about your direction in life right now.

It is not uncommon for people to try to fit ourselves into a mould or try to change their basic characters to please others. Have you ever found yourself in the position where you felt it necessary to 'bend yourself out of shape' to fit into a career, job, relationship or social situation? How did that feel?

To help ascertain God's purpose for your life, answer the following questions:

- What are your core values – that is, what do you value most in life?

- What interests draws your attention every time?

- What do you cherish or treasure having in your life?

- What group, pursuit, livelihood or cause would give you the most satisfaction and allow you to live out your core values?

As you ask God to draw you toward your best life he will show you how to live it. If you are sensing that leading, what are you moving toward?

NINE

The Life Well-lived

Last year several of my acquaintances and I bought season tickets to the ballet. On the day of each ballet performance we arranged to meet and carpool, travelling the nearly two-hour drive in a minivan belonging to one of the group. We had chosen to purchase matinee tickets for the performances held on Saturdays since the evening performances finished so late that following our long drive, we would not have arrived home until nearly midnight. We all agreed that was too late. So we packed an assortment of lunch goodies to eat on the trip to the city. It was a fun activity.

On the occasion of one particular ballet, held on a bright, early-spring day, our driver pulled into the underground parking garage of the theatre and we all piled out, straightened our clothes after squeezing out of the back of the van, and headed for the elevator. We had arrived early and thought we'd have a few minutes to enjoy the afternoon sunshine before proceeding to our seats. As we entered the elevator to ascend the three floors up to ground level, four or five other ballet patrons also stepped aboard for the ride. We smiled politely at one another as someone pushed the button to start the elevator. The doors closed and the car began to rise. Then it stopped. We had not reached the next floor. For a few moments we all waited quietly, but it went neither up nor down. Nothing happened.

While we waited for something to happen we looked at one another, then at the panel. The man nearest the panel pushed a few buttons and a couple of people asked the question with the obvious answer, "Are we stuck?" There was a short discussion about what to do next. It was quickly apparent that this elevator was not going anywhere just now. Someone discovered the telephone number to call in case of emergency and several of us reached for cell phones to dial it.

There were three men and six or seven women present in the elevator. The men wanted to take charge and solve the problem. One jumped up and down a few times prompting gasps from some of the other passengers. Another managed to contact the elevator company and shouted our location and the details of our predicament into his cell phone.

As the minutes wore on, I noticed that one of the women had tears flowing down her cheeks. Her solicitous husband stroked her sleeve and spoke to her in low tones to help calm her noticeably growing agitation. As I glanced around at the other faces, I observed that another woman had begun to tear up and tremble and the face of a third had become covered with purplish blotches. A sheen of perspiration had broken out on her forehead and upper lip and her breathing was shallow and swift. One of the men began to fidget with his keys while glancing repeatedly at the lit numbers above the sliding door. He took a deep breath, held it then let it out with a whoosh, while running a finger around the inside of his collar.

I viewed all of these reactions with interest. I knew that I would not spend the remainder of my days inside an elevator in a parking garage in Vancouver. There are procedures in place to deal with elevator breakdowns, and by this time the disruption had been reported and help was on the way. I also knew that God promises to be an ever-present help in times of trouble, so I was not concerned.

In the meantime, another ballet patron came along from the parking garage, pushed the button on another floor to summon the elevator and unknowingly signalled our car to start moving again. In a few moments we all stepped out into the spring sunshine none the worse for our little adventure - except for the four or five members of the group who were visibly shaken by the experience.

This "up close and personal" experience made me think: What is it that causes a normal, functioning human being to come completely unglued after only a few minutes in a stuck elevator? Why would a person who can handle most of the stuff life throws at her, dissolve into tears or hyperventilate to the point of passing out from merely standing in a confined space a little longer than expected? What is going through the minds of people that would cause such extreme physical and emotional pain in a mildly alarming situation?

Many people's response to troublesome situations is based not on any real danger, but rather on something else playing in their minds. Rather like the programs that are running in the background of your computer while you surf the net, there are stories and themes playing in our subconscious minds while we go through our days. These messages lie in your subconscious mind, waiting for the exact trigger to be pulled, then they click into motion and you begin to act out their programming.

For instance, why do some folks secure their homes and belongings like they held the contents of Fort Knox while others have never locked the front door of their house in their entire lives? Why would someone take the train clear across the continent, enduring days and nights of discomfort, rather than step inside an airplane that would get them to their destination in a matter of hours? There are people who would rather die than get up in front of an audience and say a few words. What causes some people to panic at the sight of a snake, an insect or a spider, even when there is no danger whatever of attack or harm?

What about you? Do you run and hide, trembling and covering your ears, when the thunder rolls and lightning streaks across the sky? If you had the opportunity to enjoy a fantastic three hundred and sixty degree view from the lofty height of a skyscraper, would you be too petrified to step out on the observation deck, or even go up in the elevator? Are you afraid to get into a boat even when it promises to be a beautiful day and your friends will be having a wonderful time sailing or water-skiing? If you travel on a subway where you can't control your surroundings, do you feel in danger of having a psychological meltdown? Would you drive great distances out of your way to avoid using a bridge or tunnel, or do you speed up when using them, jaws clenched and knuckles white? Do you avoid crowds, or find yourself spiraling into a state of high anxiety when forced to endure them?

On a more mundane note, are you worried what others may think of you? Do you refrain from speaking up when you know you should because of how others might react? Sometimes, because we are worried about how we'll look, we censor our behaviour when it would be in our best interest and that of others to act.

Behind all these reactions and emotions is one central controlling issue which has a name. That name is "fear."

Fear is pervasive, insidious and dangerous. In fact, fear itself often poses a far greater danger to your health and wellbeing than any of the myriad imagined perils that you dread. For example, a lifetime of being afraid of saying the wrong thing can debilitate you much more than if you dropped the fear, spoke up, and took the risk that from time to time you might blow it, knowing that you will get over it and others won't remember it.

If we let it, fear can control every aspect of our lives. Fear will ruin our health, steal our joy, shorten our lifespan, and spoil our fun. It can cause our hearts to fail, our blood pressure to skyrocket, our palms to sweat, and our throats to close up. It can give us pain anywhere or everywhere in our bodies. When living in the grip of fears, some people will not leave their homes or learn to drive. Some will faint at the sight of a needle or a drop of blood, while others scream and run at the glimpse of a bee.

These fears do not seem irrational to those who suffer from them, but to those who don't, they can seem almost laughable. But think of this: If what you perceive to be dangerous really were dangerous, wouldn't everyone be aware of it? The fact that fear is not felt by everyone means that it is most often merely an emotional response, not a necessary reaction. Look at the following quote by Helen Keller, the blind and deaf author and lecturer who lived from 1880 to 1968.

"Security is mostly a superstition. It does not exist in nature nor do the children of man as a whole experience it. Avoiding danger is no safer in the long run than outright exposure. Life is either a daring adventure, or nothing."

But what if a danger is real? What if the hurricane is making landfall, the tsunami is rolling in, or the earthquake is rattling the dishes? Is fear then justified? I don't think so. Fear may make you move faster, but it won't make you think more clearly or make better decisions.

When I was growing up, I do not recall being taught to fear. (Yes, fear can be taught and is all the time.) I grew up on a prairie farm in a normal family and believed everyone to be harmless. I knew that bad things happened "out there" in the world, but they didn't happen in my world. My grandparents lived across the yard from my family and we never locked our doors. In fact, we would leave on vacations of a week or more and be sure to leave the front door open in case anyone passing by needed shelter or a meal while we were gone. There was never any fear of robbery or vandalism. We were taught that God would look after things while we were gone.

Then I moved to the city and got married. I quickly learned that the attitudes of people in the city were vastly different from my faith-filled, country upbringing. Many people with whom I came into contact imparted the fear of loss or violation to me. After only a few years of being subjected to a climate of fear, I had become as fearful as everyone else. I locked my front door while I was in the back yard, even though I don't recall anyone whom I did not know except the letter carrier ever coming to the house. I came to distrust strangers I met while walking down the street. After all, who knew what harm they might be devising?

I found I was especially fearful when it was dark, and after I attended a police program on safety for women, I became afraid of even more possible troubles and disasters. I began to see myself as a potential victim, helpless in the face of a world full of criminals and miscreants whose sole aim was to seek out vulnerable people like me and inflict pain and suffering. As it happened, I witnessed a couple of break-ins and thefts in my neighbourhood, and had to go to court to testify. Those incidents increased my fear of similar misfortunes or calamities happening to me. A child in the city was abducted and murdered and I began to live in fear of a similar fate for my two young children. Statistically, the media warned me, it was only a matter of time until I became similarly victimized. My fears began to control far too many of my actions and choices.

Now we all know that bad things do sometimes happen in our flawed world. People commit all manner of horrible acts, which we get to witness each night on the evening news, and if that weren't enough, they are dramatized for our prime-time entertainment, too. We could argue that the only sane response to such carnage going on around us is fear. After all, most people believe that fear is a perfectly normal response to the dangers of life. A certain amount of it is considered healthy in some way, as a means of warning us to take care, watch out, or be on guard. Fear is considered to be a normal emotion. Lots of people believe that not to have fear is just plain irresponsible.

During this time as a young mother, my husband went away on a business trip for about a week. Since he seldom travelled anywhere without me, it was unusual for me to be left home alone with the children. In the evenings I would put my children to bed and sit alone reading or watching television, while at the same time being alert to every sound outside my house. I checked and double-checked the locks on the doors and the windows, making sure that we were securely bolted in, yet I spent night after night with my nerves on edge, watchful and vigilant in case of danger. I jumped with heart racing whenever the shrub in the front flowerbed scratched against the siding. I alternated between turning the television up loud so I couldn't hear any sounds from outside, and turning it down so low it was barely audible in case I missed any sounds from outside. If the telephone rang my heart nearly stopped, so great was my shock and fear. I spent the nights in fitful sleep, my worries constantly waking me then would lie awake listening, covers pulled up under my chin, ears straining for possible sounds of an intruder.

After a few nights like this it began to dawn on me that my fears were excessive. I think that being alone brought me face to face with just how out of control my fears had become. I thought back on my childhood, and indeed how my parents still lived, never fearing, never locking the door, and never expecting disaster. I realized that fearing was something that I had learned in the previous few years and remembered that there was another way to live. If other adults whom I knew well were not living in constant fear, then it was possible for me to live that way, too.

Once I examined how fear had taken over so much of my thinking, and recognized that I could live a different way, I determined then to overcome it. I decided that I no longer wanted to be a person whose life was controlled by worry, apprehension or terror. But how do you stop being afraid when it has become such a strong habit? How do you change your thinking and rein in an emotion that is out of control? It was not enough to try only to remove fear from my set of reactions. It would need to be replaced with something else, something stronger, completely reliable and trustworthy. It was then that I got out my Bible to see what God had to say about fear.

While everyone around me had told me that there was ample reason to be afraid, that fear is normal and sometimes even healthy, I discovered that God, in his own book, discussed the subject of fear in quite another way. I also found that, clearly, fear is not new. There were people in ages gone by whose hearts failed them for fear just as there are today. You really can be "scared to death." People throughout history have suffered from the negative effects of fear just as people do today.

"Fear not"

As I read, I saw over and over that God instructs us not to fear. I found that Jesus, in his teachings and his encounters with people in his community and in his travels instructed people not to be afraid, to have no fear, or simply to "fear not." Evidently, God has strong opinions about fear. He doesn't like it. Do you realize that the saying, "Fear not," and phrases with similar meaning, appear more than three hundred and sixty times in the Bible? That's one dose of "Fear not" for every day of the year. It sounds like God is serious about us not having fear, doesn't it? So let me ask you this: If fear is normal, why does God tell us not to fear?

The fact is fear serves no healthy purpose. It affects our bodies in numerous ways that interfere with our wellbeing. It meddles with our ability to think clearly and plagues our minds. It troubles our spirits and hinders our communication with God and others. Fear simply has no redeeming features.

Plainly, fear is not from God, or why would he admonish us so often to "Fear not"? It is easy to see that fear is the handiwork of the enemy of our souls. Since his mandate is to steal, kill and destroy us, can you see how fear works for him?

In my determination to remove fear as a motivator from my life, I had to find a replacement in order to remove it. If fear was to move out, something better had to move in to take its place. One evening, those years ago, as I sat alone in my home searching God's words for answers I came across the following verse:

"The angel of the Lord camps around those who fear him, and he delivers them."[1]

I wondered what it meant by "those who fear him." Wasn't fear already the problem? I did some more studying, both in my Bible references and with my thesaurus and found that the word "fear," though usually meaning "dread, fright, terror, panic or worry," when applied to how we relate to God means "awe, amazement, reverence, and respect." I realized that since this was definitely how I perceived and related to God (with awe and respect), I qualified for having angels camping around me to protect and deliver me from harm.

Suddenly, I envisioned tents and angels camping all around my house. I lay back on my sofa and pictured a camp-out, similar to an army camp or a scouts' camp, where there are lots of tents, camp fires glowing in the darkness and, in this case, angels sitting around those campfires drinking coffee and talking into the night. They were relaxed yet always on guard for danger. Their weapons lay on the ground near them ready to be picked up and used if the need arose. I allowed myself to visualize clearly a great number of very large warring angels, dressed and ready for battle, and camping on my lawn.

I believe that God gave me this vision to show me how not to fear. The fear that I had could be replaced with faith in God's word and his promises of angelic protection. From what I had read about angels, they are not pretty little blonde ladies with fluffy, diaphanous dresses who fly around dropping kisses on the foreheads of sleeping children. The angels that I had read about from the visions of others were tall enough for their heads to reach up to or beyond the ceiling, large male warriors whose job is to fight our battles, protect us from harm and lead us toward God's best for us.

As I allowed the vision of the protecting angels camping in my yard to make a strong impression upon me, the fear and dread of being alone in the city at night drained away. God clearly showed me through his word that he had given me angels to keep me safe and protect me, and my house, from danger or intruders.

As I got ready for bed, the fear tried to come back. Do you imagine fear is just an emotion? It is not. Fear is a spirit. It is an evil spirit, since it is out for our downfall. The way to deal with a spirit from the enemy is to attack it with what God says. Yes, that's right, attack it! Fear is a bully and when you back down, it will get the upper hand. But when you attack that spirit called fear with what it dreads most, which is the word of God, it has to leave you.

As I put on my pyjamas, washed my face, checked on the children, and turned out the lights, I repeated and personalized that verse I had discovered. "The angel of the Lord camps around *me* and protects me and delivers me." When I said those words out loud, immediately that awful fear left. But it did not want to leave, so I kept saying the verse aloud over and over. That night I slept in peace, knowing that my lawns were covered with angels who were on the job of guarding me and my children from harm.

Does this sound farfetched to you? Do you think that just repeating a few words could not change your thinking, bring peace to your emotions, and help your body relax? Then think about this: Suppose you hear of a crime that took place in your neighbourhood one night. The next morning at work everyone is talking about it. In the lunch room someone begins to talk about how afraid she is about something similar happening to her. The others in the group take up the conversation, adding their own fear talk to the mix. (The spirit of fear waltzes in and provokes everyone to greater and greater fear as they talk.)

Will you leave that room feeling more or less anxiety than when you entered? Do those spoken words have power? The answer is: yes, they do. Now, imagine if God walked in the room and announced that no one need worry. The perpetrators of the crime have been apprehended, and furthermore, he is posting extra guardian angels around each person present and around their homes. At his word, everyone relaxes because God himself has spoken. He controls the universe and keeps it all in working order, so you know that his word carries power. What he says is how it is going to be.

Here is the key: God's word has power. It has power over the enemy and it has power to push back evil. In order for God's word to be spoken in the world, though, someone has to find out what God said and then speak it out loud for it to effect change both externally and internally. When we speak God's word, it affects the world around us, and our conscious and sub-conscious minds.

Can you see that in order for any of us to find that sweet place in the Spirit and to enjoy a life well-lived, fear *has* to go?

Total, lasting change

I don't pretend to be a psychologist and though the psychological profession has made huge contributions to the well-being of many people, I believe it often falls short in bringing more than just bearable recovery from the hurts and fears that afflict us.

Only God has truly the power to change a life permanently. Only God can take something old and make it new. When you become a believer in Christ your old things pass away and you become a new creature in the eyes of God. That means that all the dumb mistakes you've made in your life, the stuff you are ashamed of or just know was wrong, all the blunders you have made that you regret, and all of the times you blew it and blew it again; these all pass from God's consciousness. You become squeaky clean and brand new. You get to start over with a clean slate. This is the beauty of total forgiveness. Your spirit is renewed. There is no substitute for the healing, peace and joy that God can give you.

Does this mean that you will have a new personality or that all your old habits and wrong beliefs will instantly be removed? No, not likely. Even though our spirits become new and we have become like a new creation in the spiritual realm, our minds, wills, and emotions are still the same-old-same-old. Our minds need to be renewed, and this takes a little more time.

You see, no matter how smart we are or how clean a life we have lived, our beliefs can still be riddled with fears and lies. Stuff happens to us when we are children that we don't understand, so we develop beliefs as a result of these events and experiences. We learn to fear and while those beliefs may or may not be true, they lodge in our subconscious minds.

It is like a seed that gets planted, sprouts and puts down roots that grow and attach to our subconscious. The plant that grows from the root is what drives our behaviour or our reactions to life's events. We think that we are just acting like we do because that's what we're like or that is normal in our experience. But the truth is that there can be a belief rooted in our subconscious mind that is directing our actions and responses.

When you decide to live a life dedicated to following God's leading, he will begin to point out to you the roots of the fears that govern your thinking and actions. He may bring you into situations that cause you to notice that you have a problem. If you don't want to look at that, he still won't force you, but you will continue to suffer from that problem until you turn to him for help. He will be waiting patiently for you when you do.

As I began to deal with my fears, God shone a light on the roots of those fears. I had chosen at different times in my childhood and early adulthood to give place to a spirit of fear and let it take root in my mind so that it was influencing my thinking and my choices.

For example, as a young child I had allergies and trouble with my sinuses. When I was about five or six years old, my siblings and I were taken for swimming lessons and I learned, to my horror that I was expected to put my head under water and that somehow the water would not go up my nose. Whether I didn't catch the specific instructions on how to achieve that, or I just could never manage it successfully, I don't remember. The result was that whenever I put my face in the water, the water went swooshing up into my sinuses causing me no end of pain, choking, coughing and tears.

It was a terrible, frightening experience for me. I failed to grasp that to keep this from happening you have to blow air out your nose when you swim. As a result of that early childhood experience, I was terrified of water. When our family went to the lake, I played only in the shallow water where there was no danger of my head getting wet and water going up my nose. Eventually, I discovered swimmer's nose-plugs and was able to enjoy swimming more, but I was left with an intense fear of deep water.

Fast-forward a couple of decades when I decided to tackle the issue of fear head-on. I had made a conscious decision never again to be motivated by fear. I knew that I had to pull out the roots of those old fears that had been planted in my childhood and young adulthood, but many were buried so deeply that I did not know where the root originated. I only experienced the fruit that they produced.

I determined to start with what I already knew. By taking note of any time when I felt fearful, in whatever situation, I refused to give it time or attention. I turned down the opportunity to think fearful thoughts, entertain fearful ideas, and discuss fears with anyone. I had drawn a line in the sand. I stood on one side of the line, and the fears were instructed to stay on the other side. Soon it became a habit to challenge and block entry to fearful thoughts. Before long, I didn't even have to think about it anymore because those old fears that had enjoyed plaguing me for so long just gave up and went away.

When it came to my fear of deep water, I never specifically tackled that fear since I never had much opportunity to confront it. Then one warm, sunny day a friend offered to take me sailing. I dropped everything, left my work for a later time, and hopped aboard his boat for my first sailing experience. Following his expert directions, I helped to sail the boat out into the lake. It wasn't until we had been on the water for more than an hour that I realized that I had no fear of it. As I peered over the side of the boat into the deep blue-green water, I thought how beautiful it looked. The sun sparkled on the waves as the boat cut through the surface of the lake. Fear was conspicuously absent. So even though I had not set out to pull up the root of the fear of water, when I undertook to become fearless in other things, I also became fearless in water. What a great sense of freedom I experienced!

God wants us to be free of limiting beliefs and fears. If we allow him to address them, we can begin to be free from them. And I would far rather have God control my life than fear, wouldn't you?

As you sit in the silence of the morning, my love pours over you. As a gentle breeze, my sprit blows over you.

Let us go forward together. Place your hand on my arm and we will walk side by side. When the way is rough I will guide you and help you. Allow me to be the strong one in your life. I will show myself strong on your behalf and make your path plain.

[1] Psalm 34:7

240

Journal

At the beginning of this chapter I relate an event that took place one day while I was going to attend a ballet performance. If you have ever felt like any of the people in the elevator for whom being stuck was particularly difficult or traumatic, imagine what it would be like if you became free of those fears. Write how you would feel or how your life would be different if you were free of a particular fear.

Were you taught to fear as you were growing up? How was fear, worry, or anxiety communicated to you as a child or young adult?

If you were to list areas in your life where fear controls you or holds you back, what would that list include?

If you realize that, as Helen Keller said, "avoiding danger is no safer...than outright exposure," how does that thought strike you?

If you have been taught that having fear is a normal and natural reaction to many of life's situations, would you be willing to accept that in spite of life's difficulties you can be free from fear? Remember a situation that you may have handled differently had you felt no fear, and write about it here.

As a young woman, I determined to be free from the fear of being alone in the city and used the words of God as my means of replacing fear with faith. By envisioning the protection that God promises I was able to be free of that fear. Tell how you can use this same information for your own life.

Throughout the Bible, God admonishes us to fear not. It is clear that fear, terror, dread, and anxiety are not from God, nor does he want us to suffer from them. How does this concept line up with your experience?

When you come to realize that fear is a spirit, not just an emotion, and that with the power of Jesus you can overcome that spirit and refuse it entry into your life, you have the power to no longer be subject to fears. Think of an area in your life where fear has controlled you and speak to the fear, telling it to leave your life now. Say something like, "Fear, I know that you are from my enemy and I refuse to allow you to have a hold over me anymore. So right now, in the name of Jesus, I command you to cease and desist messing with me ever again." You may have to repeat this whenever the fear tries to return, and sooner or later, it will give up and leave permanently and you will be free of fear. How does that make you feel?

God's words have power in the realm of the spirit and he has given them to us to help us succeed in life. As you learn to use God's words and power in your own life, you will see things begin to change. Repeating God's words is similar to using affirmations except that the power of God is contained in the words, so what you speak has infinitely more power than just repeating nice phrases. Think of ways that you would like to see change in your life then find out what God has to say about those situations. Find verses or segments of scriptures that apply to your situation and write down those words here.

In order for us to enjoy a sweet relationship with the Spirit, fear has to leave our lives. As you envision yourself completely free of fear, how does that feel?

In Psalm 23, it says that even though we might walk through the valley of the shadow of death we need fear no evil because God is with us. What would "the valley of the shadow of death" look like to you? Have you ever found yourself in any situations that resemble a valley of shadows so deep it feels like death?

How does it feel knowing that no matter what difficulties you walk through, God is always with you to comfort you and to help you come out the other side?

God is very clear that we should not fear man because the Lord is our helper. If you experience fear of what others might do to you, you need to let go of that fear. Comment on how you will stop letting the fear of others' opinions or words affect or control your thinking.

Psalm 118:6 states that the Lord is on your side so you need not fear what man can do to you. Does knowing that God is on your side give you courage? Explain.

God has not given us a spirit of fear, so fear, anxiety, worry, timidity, or phobias do not come from him. In fact, God has given us a sound mind, self-discipline, and power. When you realize that God has already provided these for you, how does that change your thinking about fears?

When we become believers, we do not find ourselves in a position like that of slaves, rather we receive God's Spirit and are adopted into God's family as his own children and encouraged to call him our dad. Tell how you feel being considered God's own child.

You can ask God to take you back to the place where your fears began and set you free from their grip. Try this: In your quiet time, ask God to help you become fear-free and see what he says. If you have a particular fear you would like to shed, ask God to point out the root of that fear then ask him to pull it out and make you free. Write down your experience here.

TEN
The Big Payoff

When I sensed that God was leading me to write this book, I had no idea how I would accomplish such a project. Though I enjoy writing immensely, as an artist and a business owner, I already had a lot of other plans for my time and my daily calendar was often filled to overflowing with activities. But no matter on what I was working, there was always this voice in the back of my head trying to get my attention. I tried to ignore it, argue with it and drown in out with busyness. Deep down I knew that God had been urging me (I could even say insisting) to write and had been for a long time.

My problem was that I didn't really know what to write about, so I began several times to create work on subjects that I thought were a good idea, only to have them fizzle out shortly after I began. At one point, I even went so far as to tell a lot of people what kind of project I had in mind. Everyone showed interest and enthusiasm so I concluded that I was onto a good thing and couldn't wait to get started. However, every time I actually sat down to write that thing, nothing came out. I couldn't get any clear direction for the project and muddling around in it didn't seem to help. It felt like my brain was made of alphabet soup with letters swirling around but none of them forming into words, much less sentences or paragraphs. I became frustrated and discouraged so would put the thought of writing back on a shelf in my mind somewhere, there to gather dust while I moved onto other things.

This lack of direction bothered me. It was frustrating not knowing what to do and having this subject constantly on my mind interfered with my other work. I spent some more time talking things over with God and waiting for his leading. Even though I've learned to hear God's voice pretty well, I am not mistake-proof. I am too often guilty of not taking time to get quiet with him and find out exactly what he wants me to do. And to be honest, even when I know exactly what God wants me to do, rather than just moving forward in that direction, I first want to know how he's going to accomplish what he has told me. It's not that I need control necessarily, but I like to have a goal to shoot for.

God leads in unusual ways sometimes. As I sought God on the matter of what he wanted me to write, I kept being reminded of stories of how God has interacted with me throughout my life. I gradually came to realize that what I really needed to write about is that God is speaking to us, longing for relationship with us, and wanted me to help guide others through my own knowledge and experience into that one-on-one relationship with him for themselves.

To some of you reading this or hearing these words, the idea of relationship or communication with God is not new. But I know that there are others whose experience has never included closeness with God, or who have suffered greatly under the tutelage of people who claim to represent God.

Because I have devoted so much of my life to learning about and getting to know God, understanding his character and how he interacts with us, and learning to hear his voice plainly, I feel I have an obligation to share that knowledge with others. As I meditated on God's direction for me and began to write, I realized that if I can help you move closer to God, sense his love and approval of you, and help you discover the joy and passion of knowing Jesus Christ personally then I must do whatever I can to aid in making that happen.

Though God never spelled out to me what the whole content of the book should be, he instructed me to begin writing. When I finally committed myself to following his lead, he gave me the chapter titles. Honestly, I didn't come up with them myself. They came straight from the mind of God. For the text of each chapter, I spent a lot of time meditating on what God wanted me to say and he has led me in what to write through this whole project.

When God first indicated to me the title for this chapter, I thought immediately that the big payoff had to be going to heaven after we die. After all, what better payoff could there be for a life of knowing Jesus than living for eternity in a beautiful heaven with him? In all the descriptions that I have read or heard of heaven (and these include what the Bible says about it as well as eye-witness accounts from people who either, have died and been revived, or who were allowed to see heaven through a visionary experience) heaven is a fabulous, glorious place. It is often depicted as so much more amazing than anything we can see or imagine here on earth that it is beyond description.

In light of the eternal nature of our spirits, physical life here on earth is no longer than that of a blade of grass. It is important to make arrangements for our afterlife as well as our here and now.

Jesus came, lived, died and rose from the dead so that our path to God would be clear and simple, and our afterlife assured. Believing in his sacrifice and the power of his name to save us from eternal separation from God is all that is required for us to get through the door of heaven.

And while having a future in heaven is part of the big payoff for knowing, trusting and loving God, it turns out that it was not what God had in mind for this part of the book. Evidently, I needed to spend some more time meditating to become clear about what this big payoff entails. I stopped writing for a while and focused in on what God wanted to say.

A Banquet

Recently, I watched a series of documentaries about Britain's Royal Family. The program went behind the scenes detailing many aspects of the Queen's life and portraying her many duties and social events. These included meetings with high officials from foreign countries, garden parties, investitures and appointments, as well as innumerable less significant obligations.

One of the annual events at the palace is a dinner for all the diplomats and ambassadors from nations around the world who are stationed in Britain. This affair is elaborate and elegant, for which every aspect of the evening is planned and presented to perfection. The servants even put cloth covers over their shoes, get up on the tables, and measure to the exact centimetre where the plates and flowers will be placed. The menu is exquisite and the guests are served with grace and poise.

This banquet is a metaphor for a life in touch with God. He invites us to a sumptuous banquet that he has prepared for us. On the table we can find hope, joy, love, healing, truth, friendship, tenderness, contentment, prosperity, well-being, health, provision, peace and more. The menu includes everything for which we could ever ask or have need. It begins today and lasts forever. The invitations have gone out. Jesus said, "Behold, I stand at the door and knock." Imagine him with an invitation in his hand, standing at your door and knocking. He wants to deliver the invitation and welcome you to the banquet. He does this for each one of us.

Yet, for some reason, there are people who refuse to come. They won't open the door. Filled with distrust or fear, they will not accept the invitation. Some say they don't have time, they are too busy working or playing, they are too stressed out or too lazy. Others refuse to come because they have been taught to hate the host, even though they don't really know him. They have decided that they will never darken his door, and to be frank, until they change their attitudes, they will miss out.

Still others accept the invitation and come to the palace, but believe that God is a mean and vindictive host, so when they arrive they refuse to enter past the front porch. Convinced of a cold reception, their belief becomes self-fulfilling since they never enter the banquet hall long enough to greet or converse with their welcoming and generous host.

There are also those who aren't aware that there is a banquet being served. Some are so convinced that God is stingy and miserly that they come with their pockets full of crackers and cheese expecting that there will be nothing to for them beyond the most meager dry, discarded crumbs. Somewhere they have learned that God wants to make them suffer and that if they get any closer to him he will see that they do.

Then there are the proud. They see themselves as equal with the host and arrive decked out in their finest. When they enter the palace, they shoulder others aside and make sure everyone notices that they are people of great importance. They hold lofty positions, which they are convinced affords them special privileges, high above the commoners huddled around the door. So consumed are they with their own importance they don't even notice that a banquet has been set out before them and that the host anticipates the respect and honour that is appropriate. They are convinced of their own self-sufficiency and power, yet blind to their own emptiness and need.

Finally, there are those who take God at his word. When the invitation arrives, they invite the messenger in for tea and cake. They recognize what an honour it is to receive the invitation for such a fabulous event and are thrilled and grateful to have been invited. These people put on their best outfits and arrive expecting a wonderful meal to be arrayed before them, a dinner that surpasses anything that they have ever cooked at home or even any meal they have ever eaten at the fanciest restaurants. They come with eyes wide open, expecting to enjoy everything that God has set before them. Very often, these people are children, or those who allow themselves to come with child-like faith, believing that what God has told them is the truth.

God's menu for the eternal banquet includes such delicacies as love beyond anything ever before experienced. There is joy that bubbles up out of the spirit for no obvious reason other than it has been placed there by the host. The table holds heaping platters full of patience that no one ever had to work to produce, and tolerance to replace possessiveness and jealousy that has been a plague for longer than anyone can remember. Next, these happy guests will find kindness both toward them, and that inexplicably comes out of them. Mercy, a somewhat old-fashioned word that combines forgiveness, understanding and acceptance, is extended to them without reservation.

At this banquet table set by our loving God, guests can also find infinite goodness. Badness may be cool in some circles, but it's not for us. Understanding the goodness of God draws out the goodness within us which, when we share it with others, makes the world a better place. Along with goodness we discover gentleness. If you have ever felt the sting of a harsh word (and who hasn't?) then you already know the value of gentleness. Jesus is the epitome of gentleness and conducts himself as a true gentleman, good and kind-hearted yet never weak or ineffectual. Anyone coming to the table of God can expect to be treated with thoughtfulness and respect – never being friendless again since Jesus is a friend for life. This is one of the priceless offerings.

Of the fruit on this grand table we find self-control. This is a delicacy indeed, for self-control is a prerequisite for confidence and success. As we continue in relationship with God, self-control is one of the most useful and valuable qualities we can possess, but it is by no means the only one.

On the banquet table of God we find healing from the battering and the bruises of emotional pain and suffering, to the healing of physical disease. Jesus has provided that. We really don't have to catch that flu that is going around, or be afraid of the cancer that runs in the family. When you become part of the family of God as I wrote about in preceding chapters, you inherit no sickness or disease and no ailments or physical afflictions that are beyond the healing power of Jesus. There is a whole lot of stuff that we are conditioned and trained to expect that we have to accept but over which we actually have authority in the name of Jesus. What am I saying? Coming into God's kingdom changes the circumstances of your life forever. In the same way that moving into a palace in the natural would change your situation dramatically, so does coming into the family of God and stepping up to his banquet table overflowing with good things.

I believe that you will never want to go back to what you had previously once you taste from the table of God.

To top off this magnificent banquet, and continue with the metaphor, we must take a look at the desserts. As though the other courses of the sumptuous banquet of God have not been enough, this course improves upon it all. I am going to call the dessert "freedom."

The biggest payoff is freedom. Our freedom has been bought and paid for. Whomever Jesus makes free is completely free. But like everything else that God has provided for us we can't experience it if we don't partake of it. What does that mean? Let me explain.

Our beliefs are what we build the structure of our lives upon. Whether good or bad, right or wrong, false or true, our own beliefs shape our lives. And it doesn't matter if what we believe is not the truth because we will act on it as though it were.

The problem is that these untrue beliefs still govern our lives in the same way the true beliefs do. But when you think about it that means that some areas of our lives are governed by lies, since if what we believe to be true is false we, in essence, believe lies. These lies that have crept into our subconscious minds throughout our childhoods and as a result of our conclusions about what may have happened to us are the very strongholds that continually cause us to have problems.

Using the previous metaphor again, we can see that if we enter the palace for the banquet God has provided but believe the lie that we are unworthy to partake, even though he has invited us to eat to the full, we will stand aside with empty plates while others enjoy a great meal. That limiting belief will act like truth and will prevent us from moving beyond it. The subconscious mind will be the deciding factor in how and where we live, what income level we have, how successful our relationships are and how fulfilled we feel in what we do.

When it comes to turning on the light and finding your own sweet place in the Spirit, first you have to want to turn the light on. You can't and won't find freedom unless you no longer want to live with the status quo. When you decide that you want more from life, or that you are no longer willing to live with what you have now, you position yourself for greatness. Removing the barriers that hold you back means that you can finally pursue your dreams with your whole heart. Accessing the gifts that God has in store for you gives you a huge advantage in life.

In closing I share this from the Holy Spirit.

As you move away from the leading and the voices of this world, my child, and move more and more into close communion with me, you will find your life opens up like a flower when struck by the warmth of the morning sun. My light will shine upon you and flow into you; it will nourish your soul and feed your spirit. It will cause you to grow and multiply and spread beauty all around you.

It will make you strong and beautiful at the same time and you will be an exhibition of my love to everyone you meet.

Showing people my goodness need not necessarily be accomplished through what you create and what you do but by who you are through your contact with me. The more time you spend with me and the more you hear and heed my voice the more your life will become an example of me.

As you seek my advice daily I will direct your steps – every little step – just as I have promised. As you seek my will and direction for every move that you make you will find that my success will come upon you and overtake you. Don't try to make 'rational decisions' based on what you can see or what people advise you. Simply ask me. I see everything that you can't see, from beginning to end. What I have in mind for you is even greater than you can imagine and you can access it only through your close walk with me.

This simple communication with me is a delight to my soul.

Journal

Sometimes when God calls us to do something, it does not immediately appeal to us, or we do not feel prepared or equipped to carry out whatever it is we feel led to do. Yet we often cannot see what God sees or where following his directions will eventually lead us. If you have ever had the experience of taking a leap of faith, or "jumping of the cliff" before knowing if the net is there, write about that here.

In the metaphor of the banquet, tell which group of invited guests you most identify with and why.

On God's "table" we can find everything we need to lead fulfilling and successful lives. What do you feel that you most need now to improve your life and why?

If all the things on God's table are good and good for us, can you explain why you think many people choose not to come to the banquet or why they do not partake of what is offered?

Of all the big payoffs of living in close relationship with God, perhaps the biggest is freedom. God wants us to be free of limits to becoming our best and living our best life. In what areas would you like to experience more freedom in your own life?

Often we come up against blocks in our lives that time and again prevent us from moving beyond them. They may appear as fears, self-sabotage, or any number of other emotional issues. God wants us to be free from impediments to living at our best. Psychological therapy can only take us so far and often does not locate or heal the root cause of our problems. Name some areas of your life where you feel blocked or prevented from moving forward.

When you become a believer, your spirit becomes new again, yet your mind, will, emotions and many subconscious beliefs remain the same and need to be renewed as well. God wants to help us to be healed and free.

The following exercise will help you to get free of these subconscious limiting beliefs. If there are areas of your life that you continue to have difficulty or areas that you know always cause you problems, list those in the space below. (It is important not to censor what comes to mind, since we usually hear the voice of the Spirit first. What you hear may seem unimportant, inconsequential, or even trivial, yet it may hold the key to your freedom. Erroneous beliefs can be picked up from the most unlikely or minor experiences in our pasts yet as long as they persist, they control our lives. Do not try too hard to think things through. Just write down the first things that pop into your mind and it will lead you to the truth.)

Now, quiet your mind and say out loud that you command all voices except that of the Holy Spirit to be quiet and leave, in Jesus' name. Any enemy spirits must then go.

Now ask God, right now, in which areas he would like to help you become healed and free then write down whatever seems the most important or pressing.

Ask God to choose one of those problem areas now, whichever one is the most important, and in a quiet place where you will not be interrupted, ask God to shine his light upon where the source of this problem began. Write down what comes to mind.

If the memory is painful, take a moment to feel the pain then ask God if he would, right now, remove the pain from the memory, then write down what comes to your mind.

Now ask God what he would like you to know about that situation, or if there are lies that you have believed because of this situation, and write down whatever comes to mind.

Ask God if there is anything else you need to know about this situation, and write down what comes to mind.

Now ask God what the truth is about this situation in your life. Ask how he wants you to see this situation or your conclusions now.

Over the course of the next day or so, record anything you notice as a result of moving through this exercise. Sometimes, change is sudden and dramatic, and other times it is subtle. You may notice, for example, that what bothered you before, no longer has the power to affect you. Or you may notice that your thinking has dramatically changed as a result of working through this exercise. Record your experience here.

When you feel ready, go back to your list and allow God to point out another area where he would like to heal and free you. Go through the questions taking as long as you need to, and make notes on your experience or progress. You will begin to see clearly how God is working in your life to make you free.

Afterward

Living in the light of God's love is a wonderful way to live. Will you still have problems? Sure, we all live in a world with problems. But you have access to the power of the universe so that you know how to deal with your problems and move on to triumph over them.

Numerous methods have been developed to try to deal with the issue of discovering the source of our personal issues by searching through memories of past experiences that have left scars. Though sometimes the source of the problem is obvious – childhood abuse, neglect, or traumatic events – often it is much more difficult to discern where the roots of impediments lie. Many memories are buried so deeply in our subconscious minds that we cannot begin to access them, and even when we do, we cannot always see the connection to our present-day challenges. And simply discovering the source is not enough, is it?

While much wonderful work has been done, many cases studied and no doubt thousands of books and articles written about accessing the source of our limiting beliefs and changing them, few therapies are thoroughly successful in effecting complete and lasting change. Even when analysis and psychology succeed in uncovering the source of the issues that plague us, often after years of therapy, it can still usually offer only tolerable improvement at best. Many other methods that we adopt in order to change our thinking, such as repeating affirmations, joining support groups or reading books, change our reactions and circumstances with only limited success. The road to complete healing seems long and arduous with no guarantees of success whatsoever.

Working through your challenges is not a job to be taken on alone if only for the simple reason that you are too close to the patient. I know that sounds funny, but we are often the ones most blind to our own behaviour, aren't we? Have you ever had the experience of having a friend or family member tell you something about your habits or behaviour that you flatly deny, while everyone around the table is nodding in agreement?

While many of us have come up through childhood with fewer scrapes and bruises than others, none of us emerges into adulthood entirely unscathed. It is impossible not to be touched by something bad sometime, or not experience something that left a mark and created a belief that controls your life today, either for good or bad. I don't believe that anyone among us is completely free of the need for healing. We all carry around small or big lies that cause us to stumble, and trying to overcome them or make them right is not a job to be tackled alone. The quest for spiritual and emotional enlightenment is a path than many embark upon under their own steam, but really is doing things the hard way.

The good news is that there is an alternative to chipping away at our rough edges and trying to find healing for our wounds and truth to supplant the lies we believe. What if you could just shine a light directly on the root of the problem, understand how it came to be, and replace it with a new belief? Isn't that far preferable to years of therapy? How much more efficient and precise to be able to know exactly what is the source of those problems that keep causing you to stumble, fall, or fail time after time.

You see, the problem is not the people you work with, and it's not your spouse, parents, children, or in-laws. Other people might seem like they are the cause of your problems, but they are not. The way that we can know this is because the very thing your husband or your mother or your boss does that absolutely drives you crazy may have no effect whatsoever on someone else. Their irritating habits bug you for a specific reason – there is something in you that is triggered by their behaviour, some old memory or belief that you are protecting because there is pain associated with it. Whenever they use a particular behaviour it is like scratching that wound open again.

Only by shining a light on the source of the pain, exposing the lie, and replacing it with truth can healing come. There is only one way that I know of to go straight to the source of your pain and have it quickly, gently, and permanently healed, and that is with the help of the Holy Spirit. Only God knows every moment of your life, every belief you hold, and every difficulty you have. God alone understands where your pain points are and how they got there. He knows what happened when you were a child, whatever it may be, and he was there all the time. The Holy Spirit possesses skills and abilities that no psychologist can match no matter how much education or experience he or she may have. The Holy Spirit sees into the innermost being, into the depths of the soul and the breadth of the emotions.

In matters of success, careers, family, and relationships of all kinds, the Holy Spirit can help. God wants us to be healed and whole. In his kindness, he refrains from bringing up too many issues at once, yet his goal and desire for all of us is complete wholeness. Correcting our lies takes patience and perseverance, yet the Bible states that we must let patience do its impeccable work so that we can emerge perfect and complete ourselves, wanting and needing nothing more. This reminds me of something that my father once said: "It seems like it takes your whole life to get things figured out." With God's help we can get our lives figured out, we can learn what holds us back and realize victory where before we had defeat.

There is a method of prayer that brings the Holy Spirit into the picture like a supernatural therapist. If we ask, God gently shines light into those dark recesses of our past and brings to light the wrong beliefs and lies that are hidden there obstructing our forward movement and causing us grief. This method of praying is gentle because God is gentle, yet it is sharper than a laser beam. When the process is complete, which takes only a few minutes to a few hours in quiet conversation, the results are dramatic and the change is permanent. No more tolerating the same-old-same-old. No more carrying around pain from old hurts. No more believing lies that hinder and maim. Healing is real and effective and precise.

I share the following example, though it is quite personal, for the purpose of illustrating how exactly and effectively God's Spirit gets to the root of a problem and what he does with it in the individual. As an artist and designer I create art for part of my living. However, I often had a problem getting down to work. I love the creative process and enjoy the hands-on work of drawing, painting and graphics, yet time after time when I wanted to start a new project I came upon resistance somewhere in myself. Since it was important to me to overcome this resistance, I sought the help of some people I know who are skilled in this style of prayer.

We had a short conversation before getting down to the business of exploring the source of my resistance. The method is simple and when led by a trained practitioner opens the door for the Holy Spirit to enter the scene and for Jesus to reveal the source of the problem. In this instance and during the session, I was reminded of an incident that happened when I was about seven years old. I was punished for something that I didn't do; I just happened to be in the wrong place at the wrong time. The incident became something of a family joke which I never found particularly funny but was brought up from time to time and laughed about all over again. This experience had left a scar on me as a child but not one that I thought had any lasting effects.

I was wrong. Unbeknownst to me, as a result of that incident I had absorbed the untrue belief that I could be held responsible for the actions or emotions of others, and that I would have no say about when or if it would happen. Many of my actions and emotions were being controlled by that little lie that lay buried in my subconscious mind. The way that it was playing out was that I always felt responsible for everyone else's emotional well-being. Before I could do things that I really wanted to, I had to make sure everyone else was okay, or settled, or happy. If they were not then I had somehow to fix things before I felt free to think of my work and myself. This is one of the reasons that I always felt that I could only create if I were completely alone with no possibility of interruption.

When God shone the light on this incident in my past and pointed out the lie that had controlled me for most of my life, it was a complete revelation to me. Not only had I all but forgotten the incident, but I had no idea that there was anything associated with it that still affected me. The lie said that I was responsible for the happiness of others in my life. During that session, I again experienced the emotions I had felt as a seven-year-old child. I remembered feeling shocked, humiliated and hurt, yet even though there was an apology, the fact that the incident had become a family joke meant that those feelings were never totally resolved.

Once I was led to recognize that I believed a lie then Jesus was asked to tell me the truth. He showed me a picture of the incident being replayed, but with an entirely different ending. The truth, of course, is that I am not responsible for the feelings of everyone around me, only for my own. Others are responsible for their own feelings. Logically, I would have said this makes perfect sense. But that small lie hidden away in my subconscious mind overrode my conscious mind and controlled my reactions to those around me.

Once this lie was eradicated and replaced with truth, I suddenly no longer felt like I had to bend myself out of shape to make everyone happy before I could feel free to do my own work. I was free to allow others to feel what they wanted to and I had no more responsibility for their feelings. The wonderful thing about allowing the Holy Spirit to speak to you and set you free is that he sets you free instantly and permanently. Only God has the power to heal the deep wounds that you carry around, and remove the pain once and forever. Only God knows exactly what the source of your pain is, since he was right there with you when it happened. He feels your pain at the same time you do and is the only one who can completely and permanently heal you.

What was also completely amazing to me was that after the Holy

Spirit brought truth into my soul, all the pain surrounding that incident completely disappeared and has never come back. And since the results of the lie affected my relationships in so many ways, those areas were instantly healed as well. No longer could that wound be pricked whenever something happened in my relationships. Neither was there a trigger that allowed the behaviour of others to hold me hostage emotionally.

I discovered, to my dismay, that a particular behaviour pattern that had given me a great deal of trouble in my marriage was instantly changed. When something no longer works, people stop doing it. I have no sore spot anymore, so the unconscious maneuvering no longer works.

I tell you, there is nothing anywhere that compares to being free like this! Those whom Jesus makes free are completely and permanently free. But all of our areas of emotional and spiritual bondage are not always set free overnight. When we become believers by faith in him, even though our spirit is renewed, our soul, or subconscious mind, still needs work. Often we are bound in ways that we are not even aware of, yet we continue to suffer because in all our efforts to heal ourselves, we still find no way out. I want you to know that Jesus has the way; he knows the perfect solution for you and will help you to find it. I know this from my own experience and from witnessing the experiences of others. This freedom is like no other.

www.ingramcontent.com/pod-product-compliance
Lightning Source LLC
Chambersburg PA
CBHW022116080426
42734CB00006B/157